C000319861

New York City

Editorial Director	Cynthia Clayton Ochterbeck
Editor	Jonathan P. Gilbert
Contributing Writers	Anne-Marie Scott, Shea Dean
Production Manager	Natasha George
Cartography	Peter Wrenn
Photo Editors	Lydia Strong, Brigitta L. House
Cover Design	Paris Venise Design — Paris, 17e
Printing and Binding	Himmer AG

Contact us:
Michelin Maps and Guides, One Parkway South, Greenville, SC 29615 USA
www.michelintravel.com
email: michelinguides@us.michelin.com

Special Sales:
For information regarding bulk sales, customized editions and premium sales,
please contact our Customer Service Departments:

USA – 800-423-6277   **Canada** – 800-361-8236

Michelin Apa Publications Ltd
A joint venture between Michelin and Langenscheidt

© 2008 Michelin Apa Publications Ltd
ISBN 978-1-906261-30-6

Printed and bound in Germany

Note to the reader:
While every effort is made to ensure that all information printed in this guide is correct
and up-to-date, Michelin Apa Publications Ltd. accepts no liability for any direct, indirect or
consequential losses howsoever caused so far as such can be excluded by law.

Admission prices listed for sights in this guide are for a single adult, unless otherwise
specified.

Photographs Courtesy of:
American Museum of Natural History: 33, 72; Shahar Azran/Apollo Theater: 79; Bentley Hotel:
119; Café Boulud: 108; ©S. Berger/NYC & Co.: 77; Carlyle Hotel: 92; Cold Spring Harbor Whaling
Museum: 105; Cooper-Hewitt, National Design Museum: 41; R. Corbel/MICHELIN: 24; ©G. Davies/
NYC&Co.: 8; ©Shea Dean: 28, 46, 50, 54, 62, 63, 66, 69, 71, 84, 89, 90, 91; ©The Frick Collection, photo:
John Bigelow Taylor: 36; American Folk Art Museum/August Bandal: 40; ©Gioriello/NYC&Co.: 9;
©Group Photos/NYC&Co.: 9; ©Jeff Goldberg/Estro/Whitney Museum of American Art: 8, 48; ©Jeff
Greenberg/NYC&Co.: 6, 9, 19, 21, 23, 27, 31, 42, 52, 55, 58, 60, 64, 73, 74, 75, 80, 81, 87, 96, 101; ©Mick
Hales/Metropolitan Museum of Art/NYC&Co.: 35; ©John Hill/Historic Hudson Valley: 103; Historic
Urban Plans: 18; Hotel Belleclaire: 122; Brigitta L. House/MICHELIN: 4, 5, 6, 7, 16-17, 20, 22, 26, 30, 37,
38, 59, 61, 68, 76, 83, 86, 109, 110, 113, 115, 120, 124; Michael Mundy/Ian Schrager Hotels: 124; ©2003
ImageDJ Corp.: 92; Intrepid Sea, Air & Space Museum: 75; Iroquois Hotel: 118; Keens Steakhouse: 108;
Lou Hammond & Assoc.: 116-117; ©Robert Lipper: 104; Lower Eastside Tenement Museum: 44; Magnet
Communications LLC: 106-107; ©Kevin McCormich/NYC&Co.: 7; Metropolitan Museum of Art, Henry
G. Marquand Collection: 39; MOMA/©2005 Timothy Hursley: 39; Morris-Jumel Mansion: 56; Museum
for African Art: 100; Pam Dewey/National Museum of the American Indian: 47; David Schlegel/Neue
Galerie: 51; New York Palace Hotel: 57, 118, 124; New York Historical Society: 47; ©NYC&Co.: 4, 5, 8, 29,
70, 95, 97; NPS: 55; Noguchi Museum New York/©2004 Elizabeth Felicella: 99; Cynthia Ochterbeck/
MICHELIN: 121; ©Susana Pashko/NYC&Co.: 43; Morgan Library/©2005 Todd Eberle: 45; Radio City
Entertainment: 78; Ritz-Carlton Hotel: 92; Sarabeth's: 112, 115; PhotoDisc©: 113, 114; The Hall Company,
NY: 111, 115; United Nations: 4, 32; Washington Square Hotel: 123; Westin New York at Times Square: 3,
5, 85, 119; ©Weegee/ICP/Getty Images: 49; ©Wildlife Conservation Society: 98.
Cover photos - Front Cover & small left: ©Jeff Greenberg/NYC&Co.; Front small right & Back Cover:
Brigitta L. House/MICHELIN.

Welcome To New York City

Westin New York at Times Square

Table of Contents

Table of Contents

THE MICHELIN STARS

For more than 75 years, travelers have used the Michelin stars to take the guesswork out of planning a trip. Our star-rating system helps you make the best decision on where to go, what to do, and what to see. A three-star rating means it's one of the "absolutelys"; two stars means it's one of the "should sees"; and one star says it's one of the "sees"—a must if you have the time.

★★★ Absolutely Must See
★★   Really Must See
★   Must See

Three-Star Sights★★★

American Museum of Natural History
Bronx Zoo
Brooklyn Bridge
Central Park
Chrysler Building
The Cloisters
Empire State Building
Fifth Avenue
Frick Collection
GE Building
Grand Central Terminal
Hudson River Valley
The Metropolitan Museum of Art
Museum of Modern Art (MoMA)
New York Public Library
Rockefeller Center
Statue of Liberty
United Nations Headquarters
Woolworth Building

Two-Star Sights★★

American Folk Art Museum
Boscobel Restoration
Broadway
Brooklyn Botanic Garden
Brooklyn Heights
Brooklyn Museum of Art
Bryant Park
Cathedral of St. John
    the Divine
Channel Gardens
Chelsea
Chinatown
City Hall
Cooper-Hewitt, National
    Design Museum
Ellis Island
    Immigration Museum
Flatiron Building
Greenwich Village
Guggenheim Museum
The Hamptons
Home of FDR NHS
Jones Beach SP
Kykuit
Lever House
Lincoln Center
Long Island
The Long Island Museum
Lower East Side
    Tenement Museum

Madison Avenue
Morgan Library
Museum of Jewish Heritage
Museum of the City of
   New York
National Museum of the
   American Indian
New York Aquarium
New York Botanical Garden
New-York Historical Society
The Noguchi Museum
Old Bethpage Village
   Restoration
Planting Fields
Radio City Music Hall

Rubin Museum of Art
Saint Patrick's Cathedral
Seagram Building
South Street Seaport
   Historic District
St. Paul's Chapel
Staten Island Ferry
Times Square
Trinity Church
Upper East Side
Upper West Side
West Point
Whitney Museum of
   American Art
World Trade Center Site

One-Star Sights★

53rd at Third
Alice Austen House Museum
Asia Society
Battery Park
Bloomberg Tower
Bridgemarket
Brooklyn Academy of Music
Castle Clinton NM
CBS Building
Central Park Wildlife Center
Chelsea Art Museum
Citigroup Center
Cold Spring Harbor
   Whaling Museum
Daily News Building
Diamond and Jewelry Way
Eldridge Street Synagogue
Federal Hall NMem
Fire Island
Fire Island National Seashore
Flatiron Building
Forbes Galleries
General Grant NMem
Harlem
Historic Richmond Town
International Center of
   Photography
Jacques Marchais Museum
   of Tibetan Art
Little Italy
Lower East Side

Metropolitan Life
   Insurance Co. Tower
Morris-Jumel Mansion
Museum for African Art
Museum of Arts and Design
Museum of the Moving Image
National Academy Museum
Neue Galerie
New York Transit Museum
Nolita
Prospect Park
P.S.1 Contemporary Art Center
Sag Harbor
Sagamore Hill NHS
SoHo
Sony Plaza
Sony Wonder Lab
Staten Island Ferry
Studio Museum in Harlem
Sunken Meadow SP
Theodore Roosevelt
   Birthplace NHS
Time Warner Center
TriBeCa
Trump Tower
Union Square
Vanderbilt Museum
Wave Hill
Villard Houses
Washington Square
Yankee Stadium

The following abbreviations appear in this list:
NHS, National Historic Site; NM, National Monument;
NMem, National Memorial; SP, State Park.

Listed below is a selection of New York City's most popular annual events. Please note that dates may vary from year to year. For more detailed information, contact NYC & Co. *(212-484-1200 or 800-692-8474; www.nycvisit.com)*.

January

Chinese New Year Celebrations
Chinatown   www.explorechinatown.com

Winter Antiques Show   718-292-7392
7th Regiment Armory   www.winterantiquesshow.com

February

Westminster Dog Show   212-465-6741
Madison Sq. Gdn.   www.westminsterkennelclub.org

March

St. Patrick's Day Parade, Fifth Ave.
44th to 86th Sts.   www.saintpatricksdayparade.com

April

Cherry Blossom Festival   718-623-7200
Brooklyn Botanic Garden   www.bbg.org

Easter Sunday Parade, Fifth Ave.   57th St. to 49th St.

New York International Auto Show   718-746-5300
Jacob K. Javits Center   www.autoshowny.com

May

Spring Flower Exhibition   718-817-8700
NY Botanical Garden, Bronx   www.nybg.org

TriBeCa Film Festival   212-941-2400
TriBeCa   www.tribecafilmfestival.org

June

Midsummer-Night Swing   212-875-5766
Lincoln Center   www.lincolncenter.org

JVC Jazz Festival New York
Various locations   www.festivalproductions.net

Lesbian and Gay Pride Week   Various locations
212-807-7433   www.nycpride.org

Mermaid Parade   718-372-5159
Coney Island   www.coneyislandusa.com

Metropolitan Opera Parks Concerts   212-362-6000
Various city parks   www.metopera.org

Museum Mile Festival
212-606-2296   www.museummilefestival.org

National Puerto Rican Day Parade   718-401-0404
Fifth Ave.   www.nationalpuertoricandayparade.org

Calendar Of Events

Street Performers/Evening Concerts   212-732-7678
South Street Seaport   www.southstreetseaport.com

SummerStage in Central Park   212-360-2777
Jun–Aug at Rumsey Playfield   www.summerstage.org

July

Macy's Fireworks Celebration
East River from 23rd to 42nd Sts.   212-494-4495

NYC Tap Festival   646-230-9564
citywide   www.atdf.org

August

Mostly Mozart Festival   212-721-6500
Lincoln Center   www.lincolncenter.org

Harlem Jazz & Music Festival
Harlem   www.harlemdiscover.com

Lincoln Center Out-of-Doors   212-721-6500
outdoor plazas   www.lincolncenter.org

September

US Open Tennis Tournament   718-760-6200
USTA National Tennis Center, Queens   www.usta.com

Feast of San Gennaro   212-768-9320
Little Italy   www.sangennaro.org

New York Film Festival   212-875-5050
Lincoln Center   www.filmlinc.com

Race for Mayor's Cup   212-748-8738
New York Harbor   www.nymayorscup.com

October

Columbus Day Parade, Fifth Ave.   212-249-9923
44th to 72nd   Stswww.columbuscitizensfd.org

Halloween Parade
Greenwich Village   www.halloween-nyc.com

Big Apple Circus, Damrosch Park   800-899-2775
Lincoln Center   http://theshow.bigapplecircus.org

November

Macy's Thanksgiving Day Parade
Central Park West to Herald Square   212-494-4495

New York City Marathon
Verrazano-Narrows Bridge   212-860-4455
to Central Park   www.nyrrc.org

December

Christmas Tree Lighting Ceremony
Rockefeller Center   212-632-3975

New Year's Eve Ball Drop
Times Square   www.timessquarenyc.org

Must Know: Practical Information

WHEN TO GO

New York has four distinct seasons. Fall, with its crisp, cool days is the debut of the cultural season. Winter normally brings some snow, and holiday decorations and festivities abound. Weather in the brief spring ranges from balmy to rainy to frigid; in May the city's parks and gardens burst into bloom. The city can be hot and muggy in summer, but it may also feel calmer since many residents leave town during July and August. There are hundreds of outdoor events during the summer including free films, music and theater in city parks.

New York City Average Seasonal Temperatures (recorded at Central Park)				
	Jan	Apr	July	Oct
Avg. High	38°F / 3°C	61°F / 16°C	85°F / 29°C	66°F / 19°C
Avg. Low	26°F / -3°C	44°F / 7°C	70°F / 20°C	50°F / 10°C

PLANNING YOUR TRIP

Before you go, contact New York City's official tourism bureau for information about sightseeing, accommodations, travel packages, recreation opportunities and special events:

NYC & Company

810 Seventh Ave., New York, NY 10019
212-484-1200; www.nycvisit.com

To receive a visitor information packet, call 800-692-8474. Visitor information counselors can be reached at 212-484-1222.

CityPass

888-330-5008. www.citypass.com. You can save up to 50 percent on admission fees by purchasing a CityPass booklet ($65 adults, $49 youth ages 12-17), which includes tickets to the American Museum of Natural History, Circle Line Harbor Cruise, Empire State Building Observatory, Guggenheim Museum, the Metropolitan Museum of Art and the Museum of Modern Art. Buy online or at any participating attraction.

In The News

The city's leading daily newspaper, the New York Times (www.nytimes.com), has comprehensive listings of film, theater, art galleries, museum exhibitions and special events in its two-part Weekend section (Fri), and in the Arts & Leisure section (Sun). Local weeklies, including the New Yorker, Time Out New York, and the Village Voice also have listing sections. They're available at newsstands throughout the city.

Visitor Centers

Visitor centers are generally open every day, including holidays, during business hours. Neighborhood kiosks, which have both neighborhood-specific and city-wide information, may be closed in inclement weather. For updates, check online at www.nycvisit.com.

Midtown – NYC & Company's main visitor center is located at 810 Seventh Ave. between W. 52nd & 53rd Sts.

Times Square – Large center at 1560 Broadway, between W. 46th & 47th Sts.

Chinatown – Kiosk in the triangle formed by Canal, Walker & Baxter Sts.

City Hall Park – Kiosk on the Broadway sidewalk at Park Row.

Harlem – Kiosk at 163 W. 125th St. just east of Seventh Ave.

GETTING THERE

By Air – New York City is served by three airports: two in the borough of Queens and one in New Jersey. They are all run by the Port Authority of New York and New Jersey. In all three airports, ground transportation and information booths are located on the baggage-claim level.

John F. Kennedy International Airport (JFK) – in Queens, 15 miles southeast of Midtown Manhattan (*718-244-4444 or 800-247-7433; www.panynj.gov*).

LaGuardia Airport (LGA) – in Queens, eight miles northeast of Midtown Manhattan (*718-533-3400 or 800-247-7433; www.panynj.gov*).

Newark Liberty International Airport (EWR) – in Newark, NJ, 16 miles southwest of Midtown Manhattan (*973-961-6000 or 800-397-4636; www.panynj.gov*).

Airport Ground Transportation – New York City's major airports are served by various modes of ground transportation. For a description of all options, call the Port Authorty's recorded information line at 800-247-7433.

Taxi service is available outside each terminal. Passengers at Kennedy and LaGuardia airports should wait in line and allow a uniformed dispatcher to hail the next available cab. Avoid solicitations from unauthorized drivers. Fares to Manhattan: from JFK, $45 flat rate to any point in Manhattan (tolls not included); from LGA, $24–$28 (average metered rate plus tolls); from EWR, $69–$75 (average metered rate plus tolls). A 50¢ surcharge is added to all metered fares nightly 8pm–6am; there is a $1 peak-time surcharge weekdays 4pm–8pm.

Air Train Newark (*888-397-4636; www.airtrainnewark.com*) links Newark airport with the New Jersey Transit, Amtrak and PATH (Port Authority Trans-Hudson) networks. **Air Train JFK** (*877-535-2478; www.panynj.com/airtrain*) links JFK's eight terminals to PATH subway and bus lines to New York City and Long Island. LaGuardia Airport is accessible via the **M60 bus**.

Super Shuttle (*212-258-3826; www.supershuttle.com*) offers service between airports and to and from Manhattan by van 24 hours daily (*$16–$21*). The **New York Airport Service** (*212-875-8200; www.nyairportservice.com*) express bus runs between Kennedy and LaGuardia airports and Midtown Manhattan's major transit hubs and hotels (*fare and schedule information available online*). **Olympia Trails Airport Express Bus** (*877-863-9275; www.coachusa.com*) runs from Newark airport to Penn Station, Grand Central Terminal and the Port Authority Bus Terminal (*fare and schedule information available online*).

By Train – Daily service to New York's **Penn Station** (*W. 32nd St. & Seventh Ave.*) is provided by Amtrak (*800-872-7245; www.amtrak.com*) and the commuter lines of the Long Island Railroad (*718-217-5477*) and New Jersey Transit (*800-722-2222*). **Grand Central Terminal** (*E. 42nd St. & Park Ave.*) is served by Metro-North *(212-532-4900 or 800-638-7646)* trains from Manhattan to New Haven, Connecticut, and Poughkeepsie, New York. PATH *(800-234-7284; www.panynj.gov/path)* lines connect Manhattan with cities in New Jersey.

By Bus – The **Port Authority Bus Terminal** *(W. 42nd St. & Eighth Ave; 212-564-8484)* is the city's main bus terminal and is used by both long-distance and commuter carriers. For schedules, routes and fares for trips throughout the US, contact Greyhound *(800-231-2222; www.greyhound.com)*. For service in the Northeast, contact Peter Pan *(800-343-9999; www.peterpanbus.com)*.

By Car – New York City is situated at the crossroads of **I-95** (north-south) and **I-80** (east-west). Four tunnels and six major bridges lead into Manhattan from all directions; most of them have tolls.

GETTING AROUND

By Car – It's best to avoid driving in New York City, but if you must, stay off the roads during rush hours *(weekdays between 7am–9am & 4:30pm–6pm)*. Use of seat belts is required, and child safety seats are mandatory for children under 4 years of age (seats are available from rental-car agencies). In the state of New York it is illegal to drive with a mobile phone in your hand. Street parking can be difficult to come by; if you do find a space, read signs carefully, as parking tickets often run $100 or more. Garage parking costs around $6–$15 per hour.

> ### The Grid
> Manhattan's streets are In a grid pattern (except Greenwich Village and the Financial District). Streets run E–W and avenues run N–S. Fifth Avenue is the dividing line between east and west addresses. Downtown is south; uptown, north. "Downtown" also refers to the area below 34th Street. Midtown stretches from 34th Street to 59th Street; Uptown is the area north of that. Most Manhattan streets are one-way.

By Foot – New York is a very walkable city. There are 20 blocks per mile running north–south and six blocks per mile running east–west. Fifth Avenue marks the division between east and west; address numbers get larger as you move away from Fifth Avenue in either direction. It's a good idea to get the cross street of any address you're trying to locate.

By Public Transportation – The Metropolitan Transportation Authority (MTA) oversees an extensive network of subways, buses and commuter trains throughout the area. Contact MTA's Travel Information Center *(718-330-1234; www.mta.nyc.ny.us)* for route, schedule and fare information. The **MetroCard** automated fare card can be used on all systems; discount passes are available.

Subway – *For New York City subway map, see inside back cover.*

City Buses – New York City Transit buses generally operate daily 5:30am–2am. Buses on some major routes run 24 hours a day. Route maps are posted at bus stops; citywide bus maps are available at visitor centers. Fares *($2)* can be deducted from a MetroCard or paid in exact change *(coins only)*.

Taxis – *www.nyc.gov/html/tlc.* Only yellow taxi cabs with roof medallions showing the taxi number are authorized to pick up passengers on the street (numbers are illuminated on available cabs). Taxi stands can be found at many hotels and transportation hubs; otherwise hail one at the curb. The fare starts at

$2.50, then increases 40¢ each 1/5mi (or 20¢ each 2 minutes of wait time). Tolls not included. A single fare covers all passengers in the cab.

TELEPHONES

Area codes must be used for local calls in New York City.
Dial 1 + area code + seven-digit number.

Manhattan: *212, 646, 917*
Bronx, **Brooklyn**, **Queens**, **Staten Island**: *347, 718, 917*

Important Phone Numbers	
Emergency (24hrs)	*911*
Police (non-emergency, Mon–Fri 9am–6pm)	*311 or 646-610-5000*
NY Hotel Urgent Medical Services	*212-737-1212*
Dental emergencies – NYU College of Dentistry	*212-998-9828*
Jan Linhart D.D.S., P.C. (24hrs)	*212-682-5180*
Poison Control Center (24hrs)	*212-764-7667*
24-hour Pharmacies:	
Duane Reade, 3 locations in Manhattan	*212-541-9708*
Rite Aid, 6 locations in Manhattan	*800-748-3243*
CVS, 4 locations in Manhattan	*800-746-7287*

TIPS FOR SPECIAL VISITORS

Disabled Travelers – Federal law requires that businesses (including hotels and restaurants) provide access for the disabled, devices for the hearing impaired, and designated parking spaces. For further information, contact the Society for Accessible Travel and Hospitality (SATH), 347 Fifth Ave., Suite 605, New York, NY 10016 *(212-447-7284; www.sath.org)*.

All national parks have facilities for the disabled, and offer free or discounted passes. For details, contact the National Park Service *(Office of Public Inquiries, 1849 C St NW, Rm 1013, Washington, DC 20240; 202-208-4747; www.nps.gov)*.

Passengers who will need assistance with train or bus travel should give advance notice to Amtrak *(800-872-7245 or 800-523-6590/TDD)* or Greyhound *(800-752-4841 or 800-345-3109/TDD)*. Make reservations for hand-controlled rental cars in advance with the rental-car company.

Senior Citizens – Many hotels, attractions and restaurants offer discounts to visitors age 62 or older (proof of age may be required). The **AARP**, formerly the American Association of Retired Persons, offers discounts to its members *(601 E St. NW, Washington, DC 20049; 888-687-2277; www.aarp.com)*.

INTERNATIONAL VISITORS

Visitors from outside the US can obtain information from the multilingual staff at NYC & Co. *(www.nycvisit.com)* or from the US embassy or consulate in their country of residence (many foreign countries also maintain consulates in New York City). For a complete list of American consulates and embassies abroad, visit the U.S. Embassy website at: *http://usembassy.state.gov/*.

Must Know: Practical Information

Entry Requirements – Travelers entering the United States under the Visa Waiver Program (VWP) must have a machine-readable passport. Any traveler without a machine-readable passport will be required to obtain a visa before entering the US. Citizens of VWP countries are permitted to enter the US for general business or tourist purposes for a maximum of 90 days without needing a visa. For a list of countries participating in the VWP, contact the US consulate in your country of residence. Visa Waiver Program requirements can be found on the official Visa Services Website: *http://travel.state.gov.*

Citizens of nonparticipating countries must have a visitor's visa. Upon entry, nonresident foreign visitors must present a valid passport and round-trip transportation ticket. Travelers to and from Canada must present a valid passport to enter the US. Naturalized Canadian citizens should also carry their citizenship papers. US citizens, including infants and children, need a valid passport to re-enter the US from Bermuda, Canada, Mexico, Central and South America and the Caribbean (excluding Puerto Rico and the US Virgin Islands).

US Customs – All articles brought into the US must be declared at the time of entry. Prohibited items: plant material; firearms and ammunition (if not for sporting purposes); meat or poultry products. For information, contact the U.S. Customs Service *(877-227-5511; www.customs.treas.gov)*.

Money and Currency Exchange – Visitors can exchange currency at the international terminal of all three airports. Chase Manhattan Bank (212-935-9935) offers currency exchange at all of the 500 New York City branches. Automated Teller Machines (ATMs) are located at banks, airports, grocery stores and shopping malls. Most banks, stores, restaurants and hotels accept travelers' checks with picture identification. To report a lost or stolen credit card: American Express *(800-528-4800)*; Diners Club *(800-234-6377)*; MasterCard *(800-307-7309)*; or Visa *(800-336-8472)*.

Driving in the US – Visitors bearing valid driver's licenses issued by their country of residence are not required to obtain an International Driver's License. Drivers must carry vehicle registration and/or rental contract, and proof of automobile insurance at all times. Gasoline is sold by the gallon. Vehicles in the US are driven on the right-hand side of the road. Distances are posted in miles.

Electricity – Voltage in the US is 110 volts AC, 60 Hz. Foreign-made appliances may need AC adapters (available at specialty travel and electronics stores) and North American flat-blade plugs.

Taxes and Tipping – Prices displayed in the US do not include sales tax (8.375% in New York City), which is not reimbursable. It is customary to give a small gift of money—a **tip**—for services rendered to waiters (15-20% of bill), porters ($1 per bag), chamber maids ($2 per day) and cab drivers (15% of fare).

Measurement Equivalents

Degrees Fahrenheit	95°	86°	77°	68°	59°	50°	41°	32°	23°	14°
Degrees Celsius	35°	30°	25°	20°	15°	10°	5°	0°	-5°	-10°

1 inch = 2.5 centimeters   1 foot = 30.5 centimeters
1 mile = 1.6 kilometers   1 pound = 0.4 kilograms
1 quart = 0.9 liters   1 gallon = 3.8 liters

ACCOMMODATIONS
For a list of suggested accommodations, see Must Stay.

Reservations Services
Central Reservation Services – *800-555-7555; www.reservation-services.com*
Quikbook – *800-407-3351; www.quikbook.com*
B&B Network of New York – *212-645-8134; www.bedandbreakfastnetny.com*
Affordable New York City – *212-533-4001; www.affordablenewyorkcity.com*
Manhattan Getaways – *212-956-2010; www.manhattangetaways.com*
City Lights Bed and Breakfast – *212-737-7049*
Hostels – www.hostels.com – A no-frills, inexpensive alternative to hotels, hostels are a great choice for budget travelers. Prices average $25–$75 per night.

Hotel and motel chains in New York City:

Property	Phone/Website	Property	Phone/Website
Best Western	800-528-1234 www.bestwestern.com	Hyatt	800-233-1234 www.hyatt.com
Comfort, Clarion & Quality Inns	800-228-5150 www.comfortinn.com	ITT Sheraton	800-325-3535 www.sheraton.com
Fairmont	877-441-1414 www.fairmont.com	Marriott	800-228-9290 www.marriott.com
Four Seasons	212-758-5700 www.fourseasons.com	Radisson	888-201-1718 www.radisson.com
Helmsley	800-221-4982 www.helmsleyhotels.com	Ritz-Carlton	800-241-3333 www.ritzcarlton.com
Hilton	800-445-8667 www.hilton.com	W Hotels	877-946-8357 www.whotels.com
Holiday Inn	800-465-4329 www.holiday-inn.com	Westin	888-625-5144 www.westin.com

SPECTATOR SPORTS
New York City's professional sports teams are listed below.

Sport/Team	Season	Venue	info #/tickets #	Website
Baseball/New York Mets (National League)	Apr-Oct	Shea Stadium	718-507-6387 718-507-8499	www.mets.com
Baseball/New York Yankees (AL)	Apr-Oct	Yankee Stadium	718-293-4300 212-307-1212	www.yankees.com
Football/New York Giants (NFC)	Sept-Dec	Meadowlands (Giants Stadium)	201-935-8111 201-935-8222	www.giants.com
Football/New York Jets (AFC)	Sept-Dec	Meadowlands	516-560-8200	www.newyorkjets.com
Men's Basketball/New York Knicks (NBA)	Oct-Apr	Madison Square Garden	212-465-5867 212-307-7171	www.nyknicks.com
Women's Basketball/ New York Liberty (WNBA)	May-Aug	Madison Square Garden	212-564-9622 877-962-2849	www.nyliberty.com
Hockey/New York Rangers (NHL)	Oct-Apr	Madison Square Garden	212-465-6040 212-307-7171	www.newyorkrangers.com
Soccer/New York Red Bulls (MLS)	Mar-Oct	Giants Stadium	201-583-7000 212-307-7171	www.newyorkredbulls.com

New York City

All That Glitters: New York City

The City That Never Sleeps. The Big Apple. No matter what you call it, New York packs a staggering world into just 320 square miles. With more than eight million residents at last count, this glittering city is by far the most populous in the US; a global melting pot that acts as a cultural magent and an economic powerhouse.

It's not for nothing that New Yorkers have a reputation for being swaggering and brash; theirs is one great city. It's also a relatively young one. European settlement began in earnest here in 1625, when the Dutch East India Company established the Nieuw Amsterdam trading post at the southern tip of Manhattan Island. That name, which comes from an Algonquian term meaning "island of hills," suggests that the natives ventured farther than the comparatively colonists, who for the better part of 200 years remained on flat land near the shore, behind a defensive wall (today's Wall Street).

The transfer of authority from Dutch to British hands in 1664—and the new name, after the Duke of York—didn't faze early New Yorkers, most of whom had little allegiance to either crown; they were here to make money.

Manhattan was perfectly suited to global trade, thanks to the safe environment provided by the snug arrangement of other land masses around its large harbor. As port activity grew, so did colonist friction with British democracy, which granted British subjects 'virtual

Fast Facts
With an area of 22.7 square miles, Manhattan is the smallest of the city's five boroughs. It is also the most densely populated county in the US, with 1.6 million residents.
New York's $450 billion economy ranks 17th among the nations of the world.
The New York Yankees have won 26 World Series, more than any other team in baseball.
The average speed of a car traveling in traffic-clogged Manhattan during the day is 7mph.

representation' in parliament by MPs elected by landowners, famously interpreted as "taxation without representation." When war broke out, the British took over the city almost immediately and occupied it until independence.

After briefly serving as the United States' capital, New York established the financial institutions that led the new nation into the Industrial Age. In 1792 brokers met under a buttonwood tree at Wall and Williams streets and founded the forerunner to the New York Stock Exchange. In 1811 Manhattan's gridiron plan was laid out, and the exploding population spread northward.

When the 363-mile Erie Canal linked the city with the Great Lakes in 1825, New York became the nation's preeminent port and shipbuilding capital. The city's leading businessmen leveraged this advantage skillfully, investing their profits in new building projects. New York's population doubled every 20 years, fed by waves of European immigrants, who would help build the city not just with their hands but with their ideas.

The dynamism and density of New York City pushed the decision to build farther into the sky than had ever been done before. In the second half of the 20C, the city solidified its international position in industry, commerce and finance, and its skyline, bristling with skyscrapers, reflected that prosperity.

New York's growth has not been without setbacks. A cholera epidemic in 1832 killed 4,000 citizens. A fire in 1845 leveled 300 buildings. In 1975 the city defaulted into bankruptcy. Finally, the September 11, 2001, terrorist attack took 2,979 lives, as well as one of the city's proudest landmarks, the World Trade Center. But, New York City has proved remarkably resilient to such tragedies. Ambitious plans to rebuild downtown Manhattan into a model 21C city are well on their way to fruition. These plans have their critics, but in New York, that's all part of the process. The results speak for themselves.

Looking around you in New York isn't enough: you have to look *up* to notice some of the city's finest features. From the Woolworth Building's copper crown to Sony Tower's "Chippendale" roofline, some surprises lurk up there in the clouds. For the full scoop on New York's changing skyline, stop by the new **Skyscraper Museum**★ in Battery Park City *(212-968-1961; www.sky-scraper.org)*. *To read about the Empire State Building, see Landmarks.*

Chrysler Building★★★

405 Lexington Ave. at E. 42nd St. 4, 5, 6 or 7 train to Grand Central.

When you have money, you can do anything; or so Walter P. Chrysler must have thought when he commissioned architect William Van Alen to design the world's tallest building. One of the first large buildings to use metal extensively on its exterior, the 77-story Art Deco landmark pays sparkling homage

to the car. It was briefly the world's tallest building in 1930, after its architect secretly ordered a 185-foot spire attached to its crown, edging out the Bank of Manhattan, which was two feet taller. Alas, the distinction lasted only a few months; the Empire State Building blew both buildings away when it opened in 1931.

Stylistically the Chrysler Building has stood the test of time: the six semi-circular arches of its stainless-steel pinnacle, patterned after a 1930 Chrysler radiator cap, glimmer majestically during the day and are dramatically lit at night.

An Art Deco masterpiece faced in red African marble, onyx and amber, the **lobby** sports a ceiling mural by Edward Trumbull and ornate elevator doors decorated with inlaid woods.

They Don't Call It the *Chrysler Building* For Nothing

The Chrysler building is crawling with automotive decorations throughout its architecture. If you can crane your neck back far enough, you should be able to see the following elements:

- Aluminum trim
- Gargoyles in the form of radiator caps
- Stylized racing cars
- Metal hubcaps
- Car fenders
- Silver hood ornaments

GE Building★★★

30 Rockefeller Plaza. B, D, F or V train to 47th-50th Sts./Rockefeller Center.

This lithe 70-story skyscraper, originally called the RCA Building, is the Rockefeller Center's tallest and finest structure. It was finished in 1933, and John D. moved the Rockefeller family offices into the building shortly thereafter. Its strong vertical lines, softened with staggered setbacks in the upper stories, are considered a triumph of Art Deco design. To see them without breaking your neck, go to the Channel Gardens on the other side of the skating rink and look up, up, up. *(For more on Rockefeller Center, see Landmarks).*

Observatory★★ – *212-698-2000. Open daily 8am–midnight. $17.50.* Reopened in late 2005 after a $75 million renovation, **Top of the Rock** contains exhibits on the history of the building as well as an open-air platform on the 70th floor with spectacular 360-degree views of the city.

Rainbow Grill – *212-632-5101. Open daily 5pm–midnight. Jacket required; no jeans or sneakers.* You'll get some of the best **views★** in the city from this 65th-floor watering hole and restaurant, a New York institution.

Lobby – The murals by Spanish artist Jose Maria Sert are actually the second set to adorn these walls. The first, by the Mexican artist Diego Rivera, were destroyed for their anti-capitalist themes. Rivera re-created them in Mexico City, adding a likeness of John D. Rockefeller drinking a martini with a few "painted ladies."

NBC Studio Tour

Ever wonder what goes on inside that little glowing box you call a TV? Here's your chance to find out. Tours *(70min)* lead guests through the network's "golden days" in radio, around the sets of NBC Nightly News and NBC Sports, and past technology used in weather broadcasting *(for information, call 212-664-7174 or log on to www. nbcuniversalstore.com; children under six not permitted).* Another option is to attend a live taping of *Late Nite with Conan O'Brien* or *Saturday Night Live*, both headquartered at the GE Building. Your best bet is to get tickets well in advance, but there are also some same-day standby tickets available morning, afternoon and evening. *Children under 16 are not permitted. For more information, call 212-664-3056.*

Woolworth Building★★★

223 Broadway at Barclay St. R or W train to City Hall.

New York's "Cathedral of Commerce" was financed by F.W. Woolworth, an Upstate New York native who made his fortune with a nation-wide chain of five-and-dime stores.

The original plans called for a 625ft structure, but after the caissons were sunk, Woolworth insisted that his headquarters top the 700ft Metropolitan Life Insurance Tower. Architect Cass Gilbert (who also designed the Supreme Court building in the nation's capital) happily revised his plans, designing a structure measuring 792 feet and one inch. The Gothic masterpiece reigned as the tallest building in the world from 1913 until 1930, when it was bypassed by no. 40 Wall Street. Woolworth paid $13.5 million in cash for the building.

On its opening day in April 1913, President Woodrow Wilson pressed a button in Washington, DC, turning on 80,000 interior bulbs and exterior floodlights to the appreciative *oohs* and *ahs* of thousands of spectators.

The granite and limestone base of the building shoots upward 27 stories without setbacks, then gives way to a 27-story tower ornamented with gargoyles, pinnacles, flying buttresses and finials. The top is crowned by a copper pyramidal roof.

The spectacular 3-story lobby *(closed to the public)* rises three stories to a stained-glass, barrel-vaulted ceiling, and is decorated with Byzantine-style mosaics and frescoes.

Flatiron Building★★

175 Fifth Ave. at 23rd St. N, R or W train to 23rd St.

Even if you've never been to New York City, you've likely seen this building before—it's a popular backdrop on television shows and movies. When you see it from the north side, you'll see how it got its name: Only 6 feet wide at its sharp corner, the Flatiron Building rises 22 stories straight up from the sidewalk, like an extremely tall iron. Other New Yorkers think it looks more like a grand ship, with its prow pointed up Fifth Avenue.

Famed Chicago architect Daniel H. Burnham designed the building, which was originally called the Fuller Building after its original owner, the Fuller Construction Company, to make maximum use of the sliver of land it occupies. Though it wasn't the first skyscraper made with a steel skeleton, it was a dramatic example of the kind of robustness steel could provide. Locals were skeptical, calling the slim structure "Burnham's Folly" during construction, in the expectation that it would be toppled by a strong wind. Such was not the case, and within a few years of its completion in 1902 the Flatiron Building was one of the most popular picture-postcard subjects in the country. The intricately wrought limestone and terra-cotta facade resembles that of an Italian palazzo, with an enormous cornice that makes the building appear to loom over the street. By contrast, most of the skyscrapers of that era were tapered near the top in order to accentuate their height and allow light to filter down to the lower stories.

Enter the Flatiron Building's lobby to see a display of historical photos, then cross 23rd Street to charming Madison Square Park and snap one of your own.

Always a Great Notion

Daniel Burnham had the right idea when he said: "Make no little plans; they have no magic to stir men's blood and probably will themselves not be realized. Make big plans; aim high in hope and work, remembering that a noble, logical diagram once recorded will not die."

Citigroup Center★

153 E. 53rd St. at Lexington Ave. E or V train to Lexington Ave.-53rd St.

This 915-foot aluminum and glass-sheathed tower (1978) is best known for its roof, which slopes at a 45-degree angle and is visible in most pictures of the New York City skyline. The building is pretty spectacular viewed from below as well. The tower stands on four colossal pillars—each nine stories, or 115 feet, high and 22 feet square—set at the center of each side, rather than at the corners of the building. Under one of these cantilevered corners nestles St. Peter's Church, which sold its land to Citicorp on the condition that a new church building would be integrated within the complex. Though it looks tiny from the outside, the chapel, with its 80-foot ceiling and generous sidewall and roof lighting, feels surprisingly spacious.

The Rest of the Best: More Skyscrapers

Bold letters in brackets refer to the map on the inside front cover.

Lever House★★ [A] – *390 Park Ave.* Designed by Skidmore, Owings, and Merrill in 1952, a 21-story vertical slab of sheer, blue-green glass and stainless steel seems to hover asymmetrically above a 2-story horizontal base. It

sparked the building boom that replaced Park Avenue's sedate stone apartment buildings with "glass box" corporate headquarters.

Seagram Building★★ [B] – *375 Park Ave.* The 38-story Seagram Building, designed in 1958 by Mies van der Rohe and Philip Johnson, is considered one of the finest International-style skyscrapers in New York and served as a model for office towers worldwide.

Sony Plaza★ (former AT&T Headquarters) **[C]** – *550 Madison Ave. at E. 55th St.* New Yorkers call it the "Chippendale building" for its roofline, which looks like the top of a Colonial armoire; architecture buffs have dubbed it the first post-Modern skyscraper (1984, Philip Johnson and John Burgee). Inside is the high-tech Sony Wonder Lab *(see Musts for Kids)*.

Bloomberg Tower [D] – *731 Lexington Ave. at E. 58th St.* Headquarters of Mayor Mike's media empire, this elegant 54-story glass tower (2004, Cesar Pelli & Assoc.) has received high marks for its light, graceful form and soaring atrium. Its upper stories, topped with a flat roof, glow white at night.

CBS Building [E] – *51 W. 52nd St. at Sixth Ave.* Known as the Black Rock, the 38-story CBS Building is the only high-rise building designed by Finnish-born architect Eero Saarinen.

Daily News Building★ – *220 E. 42nd St., between Second & Third Aves.* Vertical "stripes," (white brick piers alternating with patterned red and black brick spandrels) make the 1930 Daily News Building look taller than its 37 stories. The lobby is famed for its huge revolving globe—12 feet in diameter—and the clock that gives readings in 17 time zones.

53rd at Third★ – *Between E. 53rd & 54th Sts.* It should be obvious at a glance why people call this otherwise

nameless skyscraper the "lipstick building." Rising in tiers from tall columns, the elliptical tower of reddish-brown and pink stone and glass was designed by post-Modernists Philip Johnson and John Burgee and completed in 1986.

Metropolitan Life Insurance Copany Tower★ – *Madison Ave. between E. 23rd and E. 24th St.* This square Renaissance Revival tower (1909, Le Brun and Sons), which looks like a brightly lit castle at night, is known for its gargantuan four-sided clock, whose hour hand weighs 700 pounds apiece.

Trump Tower [F] – *725 Fifth Ave. at E. 56th St.* Rising 58 stories, this dark glass-sheathed tower has myriad tiny setbacks, many topped with trees and shrubs, giving the appearance of a hanging garden. Its six-story, pink-marble atrium holds a shopping center with an 80-foot waterfall.

Trump World Tower – *845 United Nations Plaza.* Looming over the U.N. complex, Donald Trump's 2001 contribution to the New York skyline is a slender, 72-story bronze-colored glass box, the tallest residential building in the world.

The World Bar

Sophistication and understatement reign at the World Bar, in the Trump World Tower's lobby. As if to foster after-hours diplomacy for its neighbor the United Nations, the music is kept low, the banquettes private, the service discreet. The only thing not understated here is the World Cocktail, a $50 amalgam of cognac, champagne and, yes, potable gold.

Statue of Liberty, Empire State Building, Brooklyn Bridge. Your little-town blues will melt away when you see these awesome icons of The Big Apple. Some of these buildings are lucky to still be here. For years New Yorkers thought city land was too valuable for buildings to be "marked." That attitude changed after Pennsylvania Station was demolished in 1965, and the Landmarks Preservations Commission was formed as a result.

Brooklyn Bridge★★★

Extending southeast from City Hall Park (see Historic Sites), the bridge connects downtown Manhattan with Brooklyn. 4, 5 or 6 train to Brooklyn Bridge-City Hall.

With its great Gothic towers and its spider's web of cables, the Brooklyn Bridge is one of New York's best-known landmarks. Building it wasn't easy. German-born John Augustus Roebling got the commission to design it in 1869, but shortly after the plans were approved, one of his feet was crushed while he was taking measurements for the piers. Despite an amputation, gangrene set in and he died three weeks later. His son Washington Roebling took over the project, but he was injured too, getting the bends in an underwater expedition to build the foundations. Washington oversaw construction from his sickbed from that point on. Finally, in 1883 after 14 years of work, the link between Brooklyn and Manhattan was complete: and with what style—New York at last had a world-class monument. Brooklyn Bridge ranked as the world's largest until 1903.

Hoofing it – A stroll across the Brooklyn Bridge is one of the most dramatic walks in the city, offering terrific views, especially at sunset. The pedestrian walkway begins near the Brooklyn Bridge-City Hall subway station in Manhattan, and near the High Street-Brooklyn Bridge station in Brooklyn. Allow about 30 minutes to cross the expanse.

How the Brooklyn Bridge Measures Up

- **Height** – Its towers rise 276 feet; the maximum clearance above the water is 133 feet.
- **Length** – The bridge stretches 5,989 feet, with a center span of 1,595 feet between the two towers.
- **Strength** – Four huge cables, interlaced with a vast network of wire, support the steel span. Each 16-inch-thick cable is 3,515 feet long.

Empire State Building★★★

Fifth Ave. & 34th St. 212-736-3100. www.esbnyc.com. Open year-round daily 8am–2am (last elevator up at 1:15am). $19 adults. Any train to 34th St.-Herald Square.

As robust as it is in reality, this 102-story Art Deco skyscraper looked like a mere toy in the 1933 film *King Kong*. Indeed, the image of the giant gorilla scaling the building with a doll-like, hysterical Fay Wray in his hand is burned into the minds of many.

Since then, the Empire State Building has become the quintessential New York landmark. Because of its massive footprint and its tapered upper stories, the building seems to play hide-and-seek. You can be standing right next to the Empire State Building and not know it's there, but twenty blocks, or even several miles away it totally dominates the skyline—especially at night, when its crown is lit.

Although construction started just weeks before the stock market crash of 1929, it wasn't slowed by the Depression; in fact, the building sometimes rose more than a story each day. In 1945 a B-25 bomber crashed into the 79th floor, killing the plane's crew and 14 people inside, but the robust structure was undamaged. Today the Empire State Building, including its three-story-high European marble lobby decked out with sleek Art Deco detailing and 73 elevator cars, appears much as it did when it was built.

View From The Top

To get to the 86th-floor **observatory★★★**, enter the Empire State Building from Fifth Avenue. There will be a sign inside the entrance indicating the total wait time and the visibility level. The highest visiblity level posted is 25 miles (it is said that on clear days the view extends 80 miles); on overcast days the view can be a mile or less. If you decide to proceed, take the escalator to the second floor and get in line. The lines tend to be the shortest first thing in the morning. Note that even if you have a CityPass *(see p 10)*, you still have to wait on line twice: first to get through the security checkpoint and then for an elevator. Bags larger than an airline carry-on are not allowed, and there is no coat check, so pack lightly. Enjoy the view!

Grand Central Terminal★★★

Park Ave. at E. 42nd St. www.grandcentralterminal.com. 4, 5, 6 or 7 train to Grand Central.

There's a reason that Grand Central Terminal is held up as the epitome of hustle and bustle (i.e. "It's like Grand Central station around here!"). This magical public space is crisscrossed by 150,000 commuters each workday. Railroad baron "Commodore" Cornelius Vanderbilt financed its $80 million construction by, quite literally, covering his tracks. In 1903 the city had banned steam locomotives to reduce air and noise pollution, and Vanderbilt had to either go electric or leave the city. He not only electrified his trains but, with the help of engineer William J. Wingus, routed them underground, freeing up a vast stretch of Park Avenue *(between E. 42nd & E. 59th Sts.)* for real estate development. When it opened in 1913, Grand Central Terminal was called "the gateway to the nation," but like many landmarks in New York, it was threatened with demolition in the 1960s. Thanks to civic boosters, it was saved, and a $200 million restoration in the mid-1990s brought it back to its original splendor. To really soak up the vibe, grab a drink at the lavish Campbell Apartment *(see Nightlife)* or a meal at Grand Central Oyster Bar *(see Musts for Fun)*.

Isn't It Grand?

To take a self-guided tour of the station, go to the I LOVE NEW YORK information window and pick up a map and directory. You can also print out a two-page walking-tour guide from the website. Free guided tours are offered Wednesdays and Fridays. The Wednesday tour is led by the Municipal Arts Society *(212-935-3960)*: meet at the information booth in the center of the main concourse at 12:30pm. The Friday tour is led by the Grand Central Partnership *(212-883-2420)*: meet at the corner of Park Avenue and 42nd Street in front of the Altria Building at 12:30pm.

Facade – The recently spiffed-up 42nd Street facade, of Stony Creek granite and Bedford limestone, has three grand arches flanked by Doric columns. On top is a 13-foot clock and Jules-Felix Coutain's 1914 sculpture depicting Mercury, supported by Minerva and Hercules.

Main Concourse – The vaulted turquoise ceiling, decorated with the constellations of the Zodiac, soars to a wondrous height of 12 stories.

Dining Concourse – This lower-level food court showcases locally owned restaurants. Here you'll find the best quick bites in the area, especially on weekends, when lunch spots for the office crowd are closed.

New York Transit Museum Gallery and Store – *212-878-0106; www.mta.info/museum.* This annex of the main museum in Brooklyn Heights *(see Best of the Boroughs)* mounts changing exhibits on transportation history and sells transit-related merchandise, such as wallet-size subway maps.

New York Public Library★★★

476 Fifth Ave., between W. 40th & W. 42nd Sts. 212-340-0830. www.nypl.org.
Open Mon–Sat 11am–6pm (Tue & Wed until 7:30pm), Sun 1pm–5pm, Closed major
holidays. 7 train to 5th Ave.; B, D, F, or V train to 42nd St.

To escape the hubbub of Midtown on a warm day, there's nothing like sipping an iced coffee on the New York Public Library's well-worn steps. However, you have to go inside to really appreciate what the library has to offer—museum-quality exhibits and lavish interiors that you can explore free of charge.

Carrère and Hastings designed this 1911 Beaux-Arts masterpiece. Its imposing Fifth Avenue entrance, made of white Vermont marble, is guarded by two photogenic lions, and its Sixth Avenue backyard is none other than Bryant Park. Eleven thousand visitors from around the globe enter the library daily to admire its architectural treasures and to pore over its 50 million circulation items, which make NYPL one of the greatest research institutions in the world.

Rose Main Reading Room – Nearly two city blocks long, the glorious third-floor reading room has 51 ft high ceilings covered with cerulean murals, rows of long oak tables dotted with brass reading lamps, and intricately carved woodwork.

DeWitt Wallace Periodical Room – Rich wood paneling and 13 murals by 20C artist Richard Haas decorate this cozy space on the first floor.

McGraw Rotunda – At the top of the main staircase you'll find a soaring rotunda adorned with murals depicting the recorded word.

Astor Hall – In this white-marble foyer, just inside the Fifth Avenue entrance, you'll find information booths staffed by friendly volunteers.

Rockefeller Center★★★

In Midtown, between Fifth & Seventh Aves., and W. 47th & W. 51st Sts. B, D, F or V train to 47th-50th Sts./Rockefeller Center.

A "city within a city," the coordinated urban complex of limestone buildings and gardens goes together like a sweater set from Saks Fifth Avenue, with all the proper accessories. Rockefeller Center didn't come into the world so cool and collected; in fact it was born of John D. Rockefeller's desperation to make good on an investment that looked for years like a sink hole for the family oil fortune. In 1928 Rockefeller signed a 24-year lease with Columbia University for the core 12 acres. He had grand plans for a colossal new venue to house the Metropolitan Opera, but after the October 1929 stock market crash, the Met pulled out and the university wouldn't budge on the terms of the rent. Rockefeller would pay that bill and shell out even more in the next 10 years to demolish 228 smaller buildings and put the initial cluster of 14 Art Deco structures in their place. An elegant ensemble of buildings—there are now 19 on 22 acres, linked by underground concourses—Rock Center combines high and low structures with open space, art, shops and restaurants.

GE Building★★★ – *30 Rockefeller Plaza. See Skyscrapers.*

Radio City Music Hall★★ – *1260 Ave. of the Americas. See Performing Arts.*

Channel Gardens★★ – *Fifth Ave., between E. 49th & E. 50th Sts.* These seasonal flowerbeds were named in 1936 by a clever journalist who observed that they separated the Maison Française (1933) and the British Empire Building (1932), just as the English Channel separates France and Great Britain. Benches around the perimeter provide a pefect place to relax.

A Piece of the Rock

If you visit Rockefeller Center between 7am and 10am weekdays, you can join the mob of placard-holding tourists who form the human backdrop of the *Today Show*, filmed at NBC's street-level studios *(Rockefeller Plaza & 49th St.)*. Or better yet, you can enjoy a coffee across the plaza at Dean & Deluca and ponder American zeal to be on TV, no matter how silly you look.

Rockefeller Plaza – This pedestrian concourse slices north-south through the middle of the complex. In winter it hosts a 10-story-tall Christmas tree and, in the lower plaza, a skating rink. In summer the rink gives way to a cafe.

Atlas★★ – Fronting the 41-story International Building, the monumental sculpture of the globe-toting god created by Lee Lawrie was picketed at its unveiling for resembling Italian dictator Benito Mussolini.

Statue of Liberty★★★

Liberty Island. 212-363-3200. www.nps.gov/stli. Grounds open daily 8:30am–5:15pm. Closed Dec 25. For information on visiting, see sidebar below.

With a torch in her hand and broken shackles at her feet, the Statue of Liberty has been welcoming "huddled masses" to New York for more than a century. In 1865 a French historian first thought of memorializing the quest for freedom shared by France and the US. In 1874 the Alsatian sculptor Frédéric-Auguste Bartholdi set to work on his design. First he sculpted models of "Lady Liberty" in clay and plaster. Then, for the real thing, he applied 300 copper sheets to a 151 ft iron and steel skeleton made by French engineer Gustave Eiffel (who later created the Eiffel tower). The statue was completed in 1884, then dismantled and packed into 220 shipping crates for her transatlantic voyage. She was unveiled on October 28, 1886, with President Grover Cleveland presiding over the foggy ceremony.

Ellis Island Immigration Museum★★ – *See Museums.*

Monument – Visitors may enter the monument by guided tour only; the pedestal and its observation deck are open to visitors. The Promenade Tour (*1 hour*) includes the lobby, where the original torch is located, and the Statue of Liberty Exhibit. The Observatory Tour (*90 minutes*) incorporates these attractions, plus the observatory atop the pedestal, 10 stories above the ground where you can enjoy spectacular views.

Grounds – Ranger-guided tours of the island's grounds are offered free of charge at regularly scheduled times throughout the day (staff permitting).

Lowdown On Lady Liberty

Ferries to the Statue of Liberty (*$11.50 round-trip*) leave every 25 minutes from Battery Park in Manhattan between 8:30am and 4:30pm in summer; every 45 minutes between 9am and 3:30pm the rest of the year. Ferries leave every 45 minutes in summer from Liberty State Park in New Jersey. All ferries make a circuit that includes both Liberty Island and Ellis Island. Buy ferry tickets online at least two days (up to six months) in advance. This allows you to avoid long ticket lines and reserve your place on one of the free National Park Service tours (the only way to enter the statue). Same-day tickets may be purchased at the ticket office inside Castle Clinton National Monument (*see Historic Sites*) in Battery Park; advance tickets may be picked up at the Will Call window. Ferries are boarded on a first-come, first-served basis. If you have statue tour reservations, get to the boat 2 hours before your scheduled tour time. *Ferry information: 877-523-9849; www.statuecruises.com.*

United Nations Headquarters★★★

First Ave., between E. 42nd & E. 48th Sts. 212-963-8687. www.un.org. 4, 5, 6 or 7 train to Grand Central. For tours, see sidebar below. Closed Jan 1, Thanksgiving Day & Dec 25.

The heady mission of the group who works in this complex of buildings and parks is to "preserve international peace and security, promote self-determination and equal rights, and encourage economic and social well being."

The term "United Nations" was coined by Franklin Delano Roosevelt in 1941 to describe the countries allied against the Axis powers in World War II. Afterward, world leaders saw a need for a permanent peacekeeping force. The U.N. came into being in San Francisco on October 24, 1945, when a majority of its 51 founding members ratified its charter. John D. Rockefeller Jr. lured the group to New York with an $8.5 million gift, which was used to buy 18 acres on the East River. A team of 14 designers from around the world collaborated on the design of the complex, whose concept is credited to the French architect Le Corbusier, a pioneer of the International style. Since its founding, the U.N. has grown to incorporate 191 countries.

General Assembly Building★★ – Outside this long, low concrete structure that forms the heart of the U.N., member states' flags are arranged alphabetically from Afghanistan to Zimbabwe, just as their delegations are seated in the assembly hall. In the lobby is a dramatic 15-foot-by-12-foot stained-glass window by French artist Marc Chagall.

Secretariat Building★★ – *Not open to the public.* This tall, narrow, shimmering green-glass slab (1950) houses offices for 7,400 employees.

Conference Building – The five-story Conference Building contains meeting space for the U.N.'s three councils.

Visiting the U.N.

Enter the complex through the visitor entrance on First Ave. between 45th & 46th Sts. General Assembly Building public areas can be viewed year-round daily 9am–5pm free of charge. Other parts of the UN complex may be visited by 1-hour guided tour only, held every 30 minutes Monday through Friday 9:30am–4:45pm, weekends 10am–4:30pm *(no weekend tours Jan–Feb)*; $13 per person. A limited schedule may be in effect during the general debate *(mid-Sept–mid-Oct)*. Children under 5 years of age are not permitted on tours. For tours in languages other than English, call 212-963-7539 after 10am on the day you would like to visit. Lines are usually shortest in the morning.

Culture vultures, welcome to New York City, home of the biggest, boldest museums in the US. History lurks in medieval cloisters—a gift of John D. Rockefeller—and modern tenements. As for art, let's talk world-class: the Met, MoMA, the Guggenheim, the Whitney. You could spend years wandering their halls and still not take it all in. Still, don't forget the little guys. What New York's smaller institutions lack in breadth, they often make up for in depth and atmosphere. *Note that all of the museums listed in this section are located in Manhattan. For museums in other boroughs, see pp 94-101.*

American Museum of Natural History★★★

Central Park West between 77th & 81st Sts. 212-769-5200. www.amnh.org. Open year-round daily 10am–5:45pm. $15 (includes all exhibits); $22 includes exhibits and space show. Closed Thanksgiving Day & Dec 25. B, C train to 81st St.; 1 train to 79th St.

If you think of natural history museums as places with case after case of bee-tles pinned onto cork board, this place will make you think again. A famed research facility, the AMNH is working hard to make the natural world as fascinating to today's young people as it was to those who never experienced television, air travel or the Internet. The cornerstone of the present facility was laid in 1874 by President Ulysses S. Grant. Theodore Roosevelt, an ardent naturalist, contributed a bat, a turtle, four bird eggs, twelve mice and the skull of a red squirrel. Today, only a small portion of the museum's 30 million arti-facts and specimens, gathered from more than 1,000 globe-trotting expedi-tions, are on view at any given time. But for most visitors, that is plenty. The following exhibits, several of which are recipients of major renovations in recent years, are by far the most compelling you'll find here.

Fossil Halls★★ – *Fourth floor.* Bone up on your prehistory in these bright, modern galleries, which trace the course of vertebrate evolution with 600 specimens from the museum's million-piece vertebrate fossil collection, the

Levain Bakery

167 W. 74th St. at Amsterdam Ave. 212-874-6080. http://levain bakery.com. Some of the most delectable cookies in Manhattan are baked in this cheerful basement bakery, just a short walk from the museum. Crisp on the outside, chewy within, and dense with gooey chips, these magnificent creations are well worth the hefty price tag. The difficulty lies in deciding whether to try a classic variety (chocolate-chip walnut, oatmeal raisin) or a gourmet upstart (chocolate peanut butter chip, dark chocolate chip). A taste test might be in order...

world's largest. The two most popular halls contain 100 dinosaur skeletons, set in positions showing how the animals are thought to have carried themselves in the wild. Admire, among others, the whip-tailed *Apatosaurus*, the spiny-backed *Dimetrodon*, and the fearsome *Tyrannosaurus rex*, with its 4-foot-long jaw and 6-inch-long teeth.

Rose Center for Earth and Space★★ – Stargazers, keep your eyes peeled: this dazzling new space center, inaugurated in 2000, blends cutting-edge science with high-impact visuals to describe the mysteries of the cosmos. A good place to start is with a **star show**★★★ in the Hayden Sphere *(advance tickets and information: 212-769-5200 or www.amnh.org)*. The digital program takes spectators on a virtual ride through the Milky Way Galaxy to the edge of the observable universe, using 3-D maps developed with the help of NASA. On the lower level, the glittering **Hall of the Universe**★ has a video feed from the Hubble Space Telescope; towering models of cosmic phenomena; and artifacts including the 15-ton Willamette Meteorite.

Hall of Ocean Life★ – *First floor.* Reopened in summer 2003 after a $25 million renovation, this two-story hall showcases different ocean environments and denizens with dioramas and videos. The centerpiece is a 94 ft model of a **blue whale** *(Balaenoptera musculus)* suspended in a dive position. The largest animal that ever lived, this phenomenal creature can grow to a weight of 400,000 pounds and swallow up to 17,000 gallons of water filled with shrimp-like krill in a single gulp.

Hall of African Mammals★ – *Second floor.* Encircling an impressive herd of African elephants on the alert, the dioramas here present zebras, antelopes, gorillas, lions and gazelles in their natural surroundings.

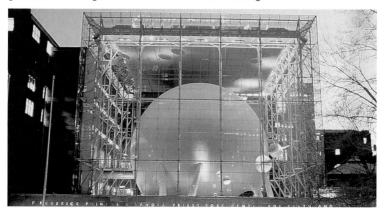

The Cloisters★★★

Fort Tryon Park, between W. 190th & W. 200th Sts. from Broadway to the Hudson River. 212-923-3700. www.metmuseum.org. Open Mar–Oct Tue–Sun 9:30am–5:15pm. Rest of the year Tue–Sun 9:30am–4:45pm. Closed Mon & major holidays. $20 suggested donation. A train to 190th St.

The Cloisters offers one of New York's most serene museum experiences. Built on a hilltop in a park overlooking the Hudson, the compound incorporates architectural treasures from Europe, including four cloisters (quadrangles surrounded by covered walkways, or arcades), to create what looks like a fortified monastery. Within are 5,000 pieces from the Metropolitan Museum's stellar collection of medieval art. The core of the collection was put together by the American sculptor George Grey Barnard (1863–1938) and was first presented to the public in 1914. In 1925 oil scion John D. Rockefeller donated 40 medieval sculptures to the Met, along with

Unicorns!

The Cloisters' famous **unicorn tapestries** date from the late 15C and early 16C, the golden age of tapestry-making. The set of seven originally hung in a chateau belonging to the La Rochefoucauld family in southern France. The story the tapestries tell, of the unicorn being hunted and born again, may be a parable for the crucifixion of Christ.

the money to buy Barnard's collection. Five years later he presented the city of New York with an estate he owned in northern Manhattan (now Fort Tryon Park), provided that the north end of the property be reserved for the Cloisters. The site is lovely to visit on a nice day, when you can watch sunlight filter in through the many treasured stained-glass windows.

Main Floor
• **Cuxa Cloister★★**, from a 12C monastery in the French Pyrenees, is the largest in the complex, but is only one quarter the size of the original.
• **Fuentidueña Chapel★**, devoted to Spanish Romanesque art, flanks the Cuxa Cloister.
• The walkway of the **Saint-Guilhem Cloister★**, from Montpellier, France, contains a magnificent series of 12C–13C columns and capitals.
• **Campin Room★★** contains the 15C **Annunciation Triptych** by Flemish artist Robert Campin.

Ground Floor
• The 13C–14C **Bonnefont Cloister★★** contains a garden of medieval herbs and flowers.
• The **Gothic Chapel★★** makes a perfect setting for a collection of tomb effigies.
• The **treasury** displays the Cloisters' collection of smaller objects, including an outstanding walrus-ivory cross from the 12C, and the magnificent *Book of Hours* manuscript.

Frick Collection★★★

1 E. 70th St. between Fifth and Madison Aves. 212-288-0700. www.frick.org. Open year-round Tue–Sat 10am–6pm; Sun 11am–5pm. Closed Mon & major holidays. $15. 6 train to 68th St.

For a glimpse at the spoils of the Gilded Age, look no farther than the Frick, one of the world's most distinguished small museums. Pittsburgh steel and railroad tycoon Henry Clay Frick amassed this remarkable trove of paintings, furnishings, sculpture and china over the course of four decades. In 1913 he commissioned Thomas Hastings to build a 40-room manse for his holdings (and himself); he took up residence here in 1914 and died five years later. Since the museum's opening in 1935, the building has been expanded twice and the collection has grown by a third.

Fragonard Room★★★ – Eleven decorative paintings by the 18C artist Jean-Honoré Fragonard, including four depicting the "progress of love," are complemented by exquisite 18C French furniture and Sèvres porcelain.

Living Hall★★ – Masterpieces by Holbein, Titian, El Greco and Bellini share space with furnishings by 17C French cabinetmaker André-Charles Boulle.

West Gallery★★★ – Landscapes by Constable, Ruisdael and Corot, among others, hang alongside portraits by Rembrandt *(Self-Portrait)* and Velázquez *(Philip IV of Spain)* in the house's largest gallery.

Enamel Room★ – Piero della Francesca's image of St. John the Evangelist is the only large painting by Piero in the US. Note also the splendid collection of Limoges painted enamels dating from the 16C–17C.

East Gallery – Works in this gallery rotate more frequently than do other works in the museum, but you're still likely to see the four sumptuous full-length portraits by Whistler.

Touring Tip

Because its works aren't trapped behind glass or cordoned off by velvet ropes, the Frick doesn't allow any children under 10 inside. Audio tours (free), available in the Entrance Hall, are packed with insightful commentary on dozens of works throughout the museum. You can also take in a good orientation film describing the arc of Frick's collecting career, shown in the Music Room on the half-hour.

The Metropolitan Museum of Art★★★

Fifth Ave. at E. 82nd St. 212-879-5500. www.metmuseum.org. Open year-round Tue–Sun 9:30am–5:30pm (Fri & Sat until 9pm). Closed major holidays. Suggested contribution: $20 (includes same-day admission to The Cloisters). 4, 5 or 6 train to 86th St.

Art lovers from around the world flock to the Met, the biggest museum in the Western Hemisphere. The collection embraces three million objects tracing 5,000 years of human history, so you can spend a day studying one period or get a primer on all of art history. The museum has humble origins: founded in 1870, it opened in a dancing academy. In 1880 it moved to its present location, but its signature Beaux-Arts facade, designed by Richard Morris Hunt, wasn't completed until 1902. Actually, it was never finished. Look atop the twinned columns—those chunky blocks were alas-supposed to be carved. A master plan drawn up for the museum's centennial celebration in 1970 called for an ambitious expansion. Wings and courtyards built through the 1990s complemented the Met's traditional exhibition halls with space for, among other things, a massive Egyptian temple (Temple of Dendur) and the personal collection of a Wall Street mogul (Lehman Pavilion).

> **Meet The Met**
>
> The Met has been called an encyclopedia of the arts, so don't go in expecting to read it cover to cover. The "Director's Selections" audio tour *(rent equipment in the Great Hall)*, which traces the history of art through 58 masterworks, is one way to approach the collection. Another is by taking a free guided tour *(offered daily; call or check website for schedule)*. The Met is usually hosting at least one blockbuster temporary show as well, focusing on a particular school or artist. Or you can just explore your favorite areas: a single wing can take a whole day to appreciate.

Best of The Met

American Wing★★★ – Spanning three centuries, the collection includes decorative arts from the Jacobean style through the work of Frank Lloyd Wright. Painting highlights include masterworks of the Hudson River school and high-society portraits by John Singer Sargent. The sunlit Charles Engelhard Court displays Tiffany stained glass, sculpture and architectural fragments.

 **Ancient Art**★★★ – The Egyptian wing is a perennial favorite, its 69,000 square feet of exhibition space ending in the glass-enclosed Temple of Dendur. On the other side of the Met, the newly renovated galleries for Greek and Roman art display statues, vases, bronzework and sarcophagi.

European Sculpture and Decorative Arts★★★ – This is one of the museum's largest departments, with more than 50,000 works from the Renaissance to the early 20C. Pieces are displayed in exquisitely re-created period rooms.

European Paintings★★★ – Paintings on the 2nd floor include works by Titian, Raphael, Tiepolo, El Greco, Velázquez, Thomas Gainsborough and others. The museum owns 20 paintings by Rembrandt.

19C European Paintings and Sculpture★★★ – These recently reconfigured and expanded galleries display one of the world's foremost collections of works spanning the 19C. It was a fertile century, and you'll see its evolution from the Neoclassicism of J.A.D. Ingres to the tempestuous work of Vincent Van Gogh.

Arts of Africa, Oceania and the Americas★★ – These spacious galleries full of stunning totem poles, masks, shields and sculpture are dedicated to Michael Rockefeller, the oil scion who died on an anthropological visit to New Guinea in 1961.

Lehman Collection★★ – Shown in rotating exhibits, the 3,000-work collection is most famous for its 14C and 15C Italian paintings.

Medieval Art★★ – Complementing the collection at the Cloisters, 4,000 works of Byzantine silver, Romanesque and Gothic metalwork, stained glass and tapestries can be found in moody galleries, including a cryptlike space under the stairs of the Great Hall.

Costume Institute★ – A magnet for style mavens, the institute recently mounted a retrospective of designs by the House of Chanel.

Drinking It All In

With 2 million square feet of exhibition space, the Met can be hard on the old legs. So take a load off at one of the museum's scattered cafes and bars. The most casual and the least expensive is the **cafeteria**, located on the ground floor below Medieval Hall. Here you'll find sandwiches, salads, hot entrées, desserts—with special accommodations for kids, including booster seats and a children's menu. A more formal option, the **Petrie Court Café** offers table service, daily afternoon tea and a weekend brunch *(dinner reservations: 212-570-3964)*. On warm days and evenings *(May–Oct, weather permitting)*, the **Roof Garden Café** offers up dazzling views of Central Park along with light fare and drinks. Cocktails and appetizers come with live classical music at the **Balcony Bar** *(Fri & Sat 4:30pm–8:30pm)*, the museum's most festive watering hole; during the day, the same space functions as the **Balcony Café**, offering salads, sandwiches and desserts.

Museum of Modern Art (MoMA)★★★

11 W. 53rd St., between Fifth & Sixth Aves. 212-708-9400. www.moma.org. Open year-round Wed–Mon 10:30am–5:30pm (Fri until 8pm). Closed Tue, Wed, Thanksgiving Day & Dec 25. $20 (free Fri after 4pm). E or V train to Fifth Ave.-53rd St.

MoMA dazzles visitors with its vast, open floor plan, delightful restaurants, and, of course, unparalleled collection of modern art—including some of the world's most famous paintings. The museum was founded in 1929 by three wealthy, forward-thinking women—Abby Aldrich Rockefeller, Lillie P. Bliss, and Mary Quinn Sullivan. Over the next decade, founding director Alfred H. Barr Jr. shaped MoMA's philosophy, mounting shows of daring new paintings as well as photography, architecture and design, none of which were considered legitimate art forms at the time. Since then MoMA's holdings have grown to encompass almost 200,000 objects from the mid-19C to the present. The six collecting areas are:

Painting and Sculpture★★★ – MoMA owns many of the most famous modern artworks in the world, including Van Gogh's *Starry Night*, Monet's *Waterlilies*, Picasso's *Les Demoiselles d'Avignon*, Salvador Dali's *Persistence of Memory*, Andrew Wyeth's *Christina's World*, and Andy Warhol's *Campbell's Soup Cans*.

Architecture and Design★★ – Includes Frank Lloyd Wright and Mies van der Rohe models, Bauhaus furniture, Tiffany glass, Russian Constructivist posters.

Film and Media – 20,000 silent, experimental, animated, documentary and feature films and stills.

Photography★★ – 25,000 works surveying the history of photography.

Drawings★ – More than 7,000 works, from Dada to the Russian avant-garde.

Prints and Illustrated Books★ – Bibliographic arts and printmaking, including the graphic arts of Picasso.

Dining at MoMA

MoMA's three eateries take an artful approach to museum food. **The Modern** is the fanciest of the three, presenting excellent contemporary cuisine in a sleek, Bauhaus-inspired dining room overlooking the sculpture garden *(reservations recommended: 212-333-1220)*. Open past museum hours due to its separate entrance on West 53rd Street, the Modern also has a more casual Bar Room and seasonal terrace. On the second floor of the museum, **Cafe 2** is a stylish rustic Italian diner, serving panini and handmade pastas. In a small space overlooking the sculpture garden, **Terrace 5** offers sumptuous gourmet desserts and "savory bites" like marinated olives, smoked salmon and artisanal cheese, along with cocktails, wine and espresso drinks. For kids, there's hot chocolate, chocolate milk and rootbeer floats.

American Folk Art Museum ★★

[M4] *on the map on inside front cover. 45 W. 53rd St., between Fifth & Sixth Aves. 212-265-1040. www.folkartmuseum.org. Open Tue–Sun 10:30am–5:30pm (Fri until 7:30pm). Closed Mon & major holidays. $9 (free Fri 5:30–7:30pm). E, F or V train to Fifth Ave.*

Defined as any work by an untrained artist, folk art can be as functional as a weather vane or as odd as a sculpture made from chicken bones. You'll find both at this provocative museum, newly installed in an ingenious, seven-story, metal-clad structure (2001, Tod Williams & Billie Tsien) hard against the Museum of Modern Art. Above the entrance, a column of glass panels is set at a sharp angle to the metal facade, like a half-open door letting in a long shaft of light. Inside, a narrow corridor opens into a vast atrium around which the museum's formidable collections are arrayed both on the walls and in specially designed niches in the stairwells.

The bilevel permanent exhibit, "Folk Art Revealed," comprising 150 works from the 6,000-piece permanent collection, challenges viewers to consider the folk art's function and the persistence of certain themes. Patriotic symbols are a mainstay of the form, ranging from a wooden gate painted with the American flag in 1876, to a red, white, and blue "freedom quilt" made by an African-American artist facing racism in the South in the 1960s. Other folk art is utilitarian yet beautiful: the massive wooden tooth that serves as a dentist's shingle, the ship's figurehead, the Shaker cupboard. What captures the imagination are the wildly idiosyncratic expressions that grow out of deprivation and mental illness, such as the romantic storybooks by recluse Henry Darger. A recent exhibit featured nearly 100 vivid drawings by Martin Ramirez (1895–1963), the first major show of his work.

Touring Tip

Museum-hopping in Manhattan can induce a bad case of sticker shock. MoMA's $20 admission fee, the highest in town, is especially hard to swallow for many art lovers. That's why visitors to New York should keep in mind places like the American Folk Art Museum, right next door to MoMA. Not only are the crowds more manageable, but the $9 admission fee leaves plenty in your wallet for other activities. For the best deal of all, visit on a Friday afternoon: MoMA is free from 4pm to 8pm, and the American Folk Art Museum is free from 5:30pm to 7:30pm.

Cooper-Hewitt, National Design Museum★★

2 E. 91st St. at Fifth Ave. 212-849-8400. www.cooperhewitt.org. Open year-round Mon–Fri 10am–5pm (Fri until 9pm), Sat 10am–6pm, Sun noon–6pm. Closed major holidays. $15. 4, 5 or 6 train to 86th St.

Founded by Sarah, Eleanor and Amy Hewitt—grand-daughters of industrialist Peter Cooper—this eclectic museum shows how artists across cultures and centuries have enhanced everyday objects. Visitors also get a de facto house tour, as the museum is situated in the sumptuous, 64-room mansion that once belonged to steel baron Andrew Carnegie. Be sure to at least step into the foyer, which is covered in magnificent woodwork. Interestingly, at the time of its completion in 1902, the house was surrounded by farms and shanties. By the time Carnegie died in 1919, Fifth Avenue was the city's smartest address.

Collection – An affiliate of the Smithsonian Institution, the Cooper-Hewitt owns more than 250,000 objects related to the art, craft and commerce of design. The prints and drawings collection is particularly robust, with works by 15C Italian master Andrea Mantegna, Americans Frederic Church and Winslow Homer, and Italian surrealist Giorgio de Chirico. Other highlights include an assortment of 18C and 19C birdcages, 10,000 wall coverings, 45 pieces of Roman-Syrian glass, and 1,000 embroidery samplers dating from the 17C to the 19C.

Visit – The vast majority of the museum's 9,000 square feet of gallery space is devoted to major temporary exhibitions. One recent show explored the Rococo movement and its revivals. Another looked at how 19C landscape masterpieces were used to promote tourism to, and in some ways destroy, the pristine places they depicted.

National Design Triennial

Following in the footsteps of the famous (or infamous) Whitney Biennial, just a few blocks away at the Whitney Museum of American Art, the Cooper-Hewitt now has a major exhibition every three years to showcase the work of contemporary designers. The results are quite ingenious. Eighty-seven designers and firms were chosen to participate in the 2006 triennial, with works ranging from prefabricated houses to robots. Expect more suprises in December 2009.

Ellis Island Immigration Museum ★★

On Ellis Island in New York Harbor; for ferry information, see Landmarks/Statue of Liberty. 212-363-3200. www.ellisisland.com or www.nps.gov/elis. Open year-round daily 9:30am–5:15pm. Closed Dec 25.

Hate waiting in lines? Imagine being among the 5,000 newly arrived immigrants who were processed here every day between 1900 and 1924. Today the grandly refurbished processing center takes visitors on a journey through that painstaking process and stands as a testament to what it means to start life over in a new land.

Ellis Island stands in New York Harbor approximately halfway between lower Manhattan and the Statue of Liberty and was a natural portal to the new world. A whopping twelve million people took their first step on American soil here. The island was declared part of the Statue of Liberty National Monument in 1965, and after a $156 million restoration program, the 200,000-square-foot Ellis Island Immigration Museum was opened in 1990. The French Renaissance building is the only one of the island's 33 structures accessible to the public.

First floor – Visitors coming off the ferry enter the baggage room, where immigrants were separated, sometimes forever, from their belongings.

Second floor – The sweeping Registry Room/Great Hall, capped with a vaulted ceiling of 28,000 interlocking tiles, was the site of initial inspections.

Third floor – Exhibits include keepsakes from immigrants and their families, and a dorm room re-creating the cramped conditions of life on the island.

Visiting Ellis Island

To get the full experience of Ellis Island, it's helpful to attend a film or performance showing what actually happened here. Free tickets to the 30-minute documentary *Island of Hope, Island of Tears* are distributed on a first-come, first-served basis; shows fill up quickly, so pick up your tickets as soon as you arrive. There are also regularly scheduled theater pieces performed at the museum; some of them dramatizing aspects of Ellis Island history. Recent productions have included "Irving Berlin's America," "Bela Lugosi and the Legend of Dracula," and "The Titanic: A Survivor's Story." Show times are posted at the Information Desk, where tickets *($3)* may be purchased.

Guggenheim Museum★★

1071 Fifth Ave., between E. 88th & E. 89th Sts. 212-423-3500. www.guggenheim.org.
Open Fri–Wed 10am–5:45pm (Fri until 8pm). Closed Dec 25. $15. 4, 5 or 6 train to 86th St.

Frank Lloyd Wright's spiraling Modernist statement—one of the most original buildings in the US—is reason enough to check out the Guggenheim, also home to some fine modern and contemporary art. **Solomon R. Guggenheim** (1861–1949), heir to a vast mining fortune, started his collection with Old Masters, but in the early 20C shifted his focus to nonrepresen-

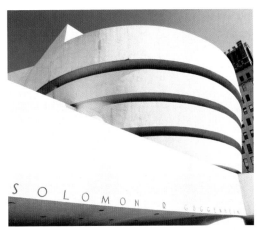

tational art. In 1943 Frank Lloyd Wright was commissioned to design a permanent home for Guggenheim's collection. Wright was an outspoken critic of New York architecture, and the city returned the favor by blasting his design. The 1959 structure, an idiosyncratic composition based on a complex trigonometric spiral, clashed with the sedate brownstones of the Upper East Side and was a nightmare to construct. Worse, its interior ramp and sloping walls made presenting and viewing art difficult, if not impossible. Wright considered it his crowning achievement. In 1992 a 10-story limestone annex was built behind the structure, with ramps leading from Wright's nautilus into more hospitable gallery spaces.

Collection – The Guggenheim Foundation owns about 6,000 paintings, sculptures and works on paper. Core holdings comprise 195 works by Wassily Kandinsky—the largest group of his works in the US—and more than 75 pieces by Klee, Chagall, Delaunay, Dubuffet and Mondrian. However, the only works permanently on display are selections from the **Thannhauser Collection★** of late-19C and early-20C art, including paintings by Picasso, Cézanne, Degas, Manet, Pissarro and Van Gogh. The rest of the museum is devoted to temporary shows.

Guggenheim Goes Global

The Guggenheim has seen the value in expanding. It has also learned the risks. After the museum opened its hugely successful Bilbao outpost, designed by Frank Gehry, in 1997, hundreds of cities clamored for a Guggenheim of their own. Berlin, Venice and Las Vegas each got one; then the money dried up. In 2003 it looked as if the rough patch was ending when the mayor of Rio de Janeiro, Brazil, signed on for a Guggenheim. But the project was soon bogged down in court, and two years later, no progress had been made. Undaunted, the museum is pressing forward in Guadalajara, Mexico.

Lower East Side Tenement Museum★★

97 Orchard St. at Broome St. 212-431-0233. www.tenement.org. Visitor center open Mon–Fri 11am–6pm (Mon until 5:30pm); Sat & Sun 10:45am–6pm. Tenements may be visited by 1hr guided tour only (see Touring Tip, below). F train to Delancey St.

If Ellis Island recounts chapter one of the American immigrant experience, this remarkable museum recounts chapter two—out loud and in person. Tour guides interpret several generations of immigrant life at 97 Orchard Street, a five-story tenement building (now a National Historic Landmark) in the heart of what was once the most densely populated neighborhood in the US.

Between 1863 and 1935, some 7,000 people lived in this single structure alone. Many worked long shifts in nearby factories and slept short ones on couches and in chairs, hoping to save enough for a bigger apartment uptown. Yet, even as overcrowded as the Lower East Side was at that time, there was also a powerful sense of community. Guides use sociological data, keepsakes, anecdotes, photographs, newspaper clippings, architectural details, and historical recordings to show how a few families got along.

Getting By: Immigrants Weathering Hard Times – This tour brings visitors into the apartments of the German-Jewish Gumpertz family in the 1870s and the Sicilian-Catholic Baldizzi family in the 1930s.

Piecing It Together: Immigrants in the Garment Industry – During this tour, visitors get to know two Jewish families affiliated with the garment industry circa 1897 and 1918.

Confino Living History – Especially designed for families with kids, the tour explores the apartment once occupied by the Confinos, Sephardic Jews who emigrated to the US from Turkey in the 1900s. A guide acting as the family's sassy teenage daughter tells stories and answers questions. *See Musts for Kids.*

Touring Tip

Docent-led tours of the tenement (the only way to see it) leave daily from the visitor center. Tickets are $17. Advance tickets, which are highly recommended, can be purchased through TicketWeb *(800-965-4827; www.ticketweb.com)* prior to 9am the day of the tour. Same-day tickets, if available, can be purchased at the visitor center.

Morgan Library★★

225 Madison Ave. at 36th St. 212-685-0008. www.themorgan.org. Open Tue–Fri 10:30am–5pm (Fri until 9pm); Sat 10am–6pm; Sun 11am–6pm. $12. 6 train to 33rd St.

To see Beethoven's Violin Sonata No. 10 in G Major as it emerged from the composer's pen is to glimpse a mind furiously engaged at work. The Morgan has thousands of such one-of-a-kind masterpieces. The collection of rare books, manuscripts, drawings, paintings, seals and letters grew out of the personal holdings of wealthy financier **Pierpont Morgan** (1837–1913). In 1902 he commissioned the noted firm McKim, Mead, and White to build a home for his growing "library." The Italian Renaissance main building, constructed of Tennessee marble blocks, was completed in 1906 and opened to the public after Morgan's death in 1913. An annex was added in 1928. The third building on the site, the brownstone where Pierpont Morgan's son J.P. once lived, dates to 1852. A major expansion and renovation by Renzo Piano, completed in 2006, doubled the exhibition space and drew rave reviews for its unifying composition of glass and steel pavilions.

The Collection – Highlights include the country's largest and finest collection of Rembrandt etchings, three Gutenberg bibles and Henry David Thoreau's journal. Rotating exhibits might present drawings by Leonardo and Degas; original scores by Mahler and Schubert; and handwritten manuscripts by Dickens, Twain and Jane Austen.

Museum of the City of New York★★

1220 Fifth Ave. at E. 103rd St. 212-534-1672. www.mcny.org. Open year-round Tue–Sun 10am–5pm. Closed Mon & major holidays. $9. 6 train to 103rd St.

The Museum of the City of New York chronicles the Big Apple's growth from Dutch trading post to thriving metropolis with period rooms, galleries, and historical exhibits. Founded in 1923, the museum first resided at Gracie Mansion. It moved to the current location, a Georgian Revival building fronting Central Park, in 1929. Since then the collection has grown to encompass more than 1.5 million paintings, prints, photographs, costumes, toys (includes a series of exquisite **dollhouses**), rare books, manuscripts, sculptures, decorative art objects and other artifacts.

Museum of Jewish Heritage★★

36 Battery Place. 646-437-4200. www.mjhnyc.org. Open year-round Sun–Thu 10am–5:45pm (Wed until 8pm), Fri 10am–5pm (3pm in winter). Closed Jewish holidays & Thanksgiving Day. $10 (free Wed 4pm–8pm). 4 or 5 train to Bowling Green.

Boasting magnificent views of the Statue of Liberty and Ellis Island, this "living memorial to the Holocaust" celebrates freedom while remembering the stories of those who struggled or died to achieve it. The main, ziggurat-shaped building holds the museum's core exhibition of 2,000 historic photographs, 800 historical and cultural artifacts and 24 original documentary films. The galleries in the adjoining Morgenthau Wing hold temporary exhibits.

Garden of Stones★ – In September 2003 English sculptor Andy Goldsworthy hollowed out eighteen boulders, filled them with soil, and planted a single dwarf oak in each. As each tree matures in the coming decades—it will take 50 years for them to reach maturity—it will merge with the stone, symbolising life emerging from lifelessness

National Museum of the American Indian★★

[M1] refers to inside front cover map. 1 Bowling Green. 212-514-3700. www.si.edu/nmai. Open year-round daily 10am–5pm (Thu until 8pm). Closed Dec 25. 4 or 5. Bowling Green.

The little sister of a larger facility with the same name in Washington, DC, this Smithsonian Institution treasure trove of Native American art and artifacts is presented inside the **Alexander Hamilton US Custom House★★**, a Beaux-Arts landmark overlooking Bowling Green, the Financial District's prettiest green space.

Visit – Step inside to view the soaring oval **rotunda**, encircled with murals painted by Reginald Marsh in 1936–37. The museum's three roomy galleries

The Man Behind the Museum

Were it not for one New Yorker's passion for collecting, the Smithsonian might not have had a museum. Over the course of 45 years, George Gustav Heye (1874–1957), a wealthy investment banker, gathered almost a million objects from indigenous peoples throughout the Western Hemisphere. Heye cast his net wide and bought everything he could lay his hands on, starting with a deerskin shirt in 1897. Crass though it might have been, the strategy succeeded in filling first his personal museum *(at 155th St. & Broadway)*, then this one, and now much of the new one in Washington DC.

branch off from this space, each containing an exhibit exploring some aspect of American Indian culture, history, or art. Recent shows included the astounding craftsmanship of the Pacific Coast tribes; and a survey of 77 works including a hand-painted set of Apache playing cards dating from 1880.

New-York Historical Society★★

2 W. 77th St. at Central Park West. 212-873-3400. www.nyhistory.org. Open year-round Tue–Sat 10am–6pm (Fri until 8pm); Sun 11am–5:45pm. $10. B or C train to 81st St.

It may be New York's oldest museum, but curators at the historical society approach its rich trove of material with a keenly modern eye. The society was founded in 1804 to preserve the history of the US, and since then it has amassed a collection that embraces three centuries of Americana, with a special focus on New York material from the late 1700s to early 1900s. Thanks to a $10 million renovation and the opening in November 2000 of the Henry Luce Center *(below)*, today the museum's holdings are presented in a more complete format than ever before. The Historical Society also serves as the world's most comprehensive collection of artifacts relating to the September 11, 2001, terrorist attacks. Blockbuster temporary shows have addressed such topics as New York's role in the slave trade and the legacy of founding father Alexander Hamilton, a New Yorker.

Dexter Hall – *Second floor.* Thomas Cole's five-painting series *The Course of Empire* and other masterworks by Hudson River school artists are displayed salon-style along with smaller landscapes and portraiture by Rembrandt Peale and others.

Henry Luce III Center for the Study of American Culture – *Fourth floor.* Presented in what's called "working storage" format, nearly 40,000 objects are on view here. Holdings range from George Washington's camp bed at Valley Forge to the world's largest collection of Tiffany lamps, with thousands of odds and ends in between. For an entertaining commentary on dozens of items in this browser's delight, take a self-guided audio tour.

An Urban Aviary

For a touch of spring in the dead of winter *(mid-February to mid-March)*, head to the New-York Historical Society, where in place of the Hudson River school paintings in Dexter Hall, you'll find a rotating selection of John James Audubon's famous *Birds of America* watercolors, accompanied by recorded tweets and twitters of depicted species. Items that belonged to Audubon, including ornithological models and personal keepsakes, round out the story of his "magnificent obsession" with winged creatures.

Whitney Museum of American Art★★

945 Madison Ave. at E. 75th St. 212-570-3676 or 800-944-8639. www.whitney.org.
Open year-round Wed–Thu & Sat–Sun 11am–6pm, Fri 1pm–9pm. Closed Mon, Tue &
major holidays. $15 (pay what you wish Fri 6pm–9pm). 6 train to 77th St.

A diehard champion of emerging artists, the Whitney also has one of the
world's best collections of 20C American art. The museum grew out of the
personal art collection of sculptor and art collector **Gertrude Vanderbilt
Whitney** (1875–1942), the rebellious daughter of railroad titan Cornelius
Vanderbilt. After starting the Whitney Studio Club in her Greenwich Village
studio, she began to acquire works by living American artists, including
painters Edward Hopper, Willem de Kooning, Ellsworth Kelly and Robert
Motherwell, as well as sculptors Alexander Calder, Louise Nevelson and Isamu
Noguchi. Her holdings outgrew two homes, moving to this, its third, in 1966.
The stark granite structure by Marcel Breuer and Hamilton Smith is cantile-
vered over a sunken sculpture garden.

Loving To Hate It

Every two years the Whitney Museum
presents a selection of what it believes
is the most noteworthy American art.
Every two years critics sharpen their
tongues and say it's the worst show yet.
The inaugural biennial of 1932 bespoke
"the deplorable state of American art,"
according to the *New York Herald
Tribune.* "Pretentious mediocrity...,"
sniffed *The Nation* in 1946. "A kind of
instant junkyard of the future" was the
Times' take on the 1969 show, and in 1993
the *New York Observer* predicted there
was "no cure in sight." Debra Singer, the
co-curator of the 2004 show, says the
negative reviews have an upside. They
are so predictable that she felt "no pres-
sure at all" to please anyone.

Permanent Collection – Now comprising 10,000 works, the Whitney's holdings are displayed in rotating exhibits on the fifth floor. Count on finding
masterworks from the first half of the 20C (Marsden Hartley, Georgia
O'Keeffe) along with postwar and contemporary artists (Jackson Pollock, Kiki
Smith, Andy Warhol).

Temporary Exhibits – The museum's frequently changing exhibits explore
daring, innovative and often controversial topics. In recent years film, video,
installation art and mixed media have become popular forms.

International Center of Photography

[M2] *refers to map on inside front cover. 1133 Sixth Ave. at W. 43rd St. 212-857-0000.
www.icp.org. Open year-round Tue–Fri 10am–6pm (Fri until 8pm), weekends 10am–6pm.
Closed Mon & major holidays. $12. B, D, F or V train to 42nd St.*

"Concerned photography" forms the heart of the collection here. The museum
was founded in 1974 by Cornell Capa, whose brother Robert took dramatic
photos of the fighting during the Spanish Civil War and World War II. Since
then the museum's holdings have grown to encompass 100,000 prints, with a
special strength in documentary re-
portage. There is plenty of room for
beauty, scandal and whimsy as well. The
ICP's vaults also include work by the
fashion photographer David Seidner,
whose portraits beautifully mimic the
composition of the Old Masters, and
Henri Cartier-Bresson, who took most
of his pictures with a tiny Leica.

Visit – The ICP devotes all of its gallery
space to large temporary exhibitions,
mounting about 20 per year. Some are
drawn from the permanent collection;
others come from other museums and
partner facilities like the eminent
George Eastman House in Rochester,
New York.

Weegee's World

The tabloid photographer Weegee
used his flashbulb to expose New
York City's dark side—if his subjects
weren't drunk, they were usually
dead. How did he get the shot? By
installing a police radio in his car—
that way he could be the first to
arrive at crime scenes, recording all
the grisly details for the morning
papers. His scandal-sheet images
from the 1930s and 1940s are now
legendary. The ICP owns 13,000 of
Weegee's prints, tear-sheets, negatives and manuscripts—the biggest
archive of his work in the world.

Rest of the Best: Manhattan Museums

Rubin Museum of Art★★ – *150 W. 17th St. at Seventh Ave. 212-620-5000. www.rmanyc.org. Open year-round Mon & Thu 11am–5pm, Wed 11am–7pm, Fri 11am–10pm, weekends 11am–6pm. Closed major holidays. $10. 1 train to 14th St.*

Buddhas abound at this stunning museum, the first Western institution dedicated solely to the art of Bhutan, Tibet, Nepal and other parts of the Himalayas. The space has cool stone floors and warm, polished-wood accents, along with a corkscrew staircase. Some 900 paintings, sculpture, textiles and ritual objects spanning two millennia form permanent and temporary exhibits; the museum also hosts traveling shows. See the "What Is It?" exhibit on the second floor for an intriguing introduction to Himalayan art.

Asia Society and Museum★ – *725 Park Ave. at E. 70th St. 212-288-6400. www.asiasociety.org. Open year-round Tue–Sun 11am–6pm (Fri until 9pm Labor Day–July 4). Closed major holidays. $10. 6 train to 68th St.* Founded in 1956 by John D. Rockefeller III, New York's premier Asian cultural center radiates Eastern calm, with a sinuous white-steel staircase, curved shoji screens, and bamboo-floored galleries filled with ancient Hindu and Buddhist sculpture.

Chelsea Art Museum★ – *556 W. 22nd St. at Eleventh Ave. 212-255-0719. www.chelseaartmuseum.org. Open year-round Tue–Sat noon–6pm (Thu until 8pm). $6. C or E train to 23rd St.* A traveling exhibition of 80 etchings by Francisco Goya and a group show exploring the concept of the bogeyman are just two of the recent shows mounted here on the western fringe of Chelsea's gallery district. The museum is also home of the Miotte Foundation, which is dedicated to archiving and conserving the work of French painter Jean Miotte (b.1926), an early proponent of Art Informel.

The Forbes Galleries★ – *62 Fifth Ave. at W. 12th St. Open year-round Tue, Wed, Fri, and Sat 10am–4pm. Closed major holidays. 212-206-5548. www.forbesgalleries.com.* This little museum was known for owning the largest collection of Fabergé Easter eggs in the world until February 2004, when the Forbes family sold them to a Russian oil magnate for more than $100 million. Many interesting objects remain, however, including 12,000 toy soldiers; more than 500 miniature boats; Abraham Lincoln's opera glasses; and the bill for Paul Revere's ride.

Museum of Arts & Design★ – *[M3] refers to map on inside front cover. 40 W. 53rd St. 212-956-3535. www.madmuseum.org. Open year-round daily 10am–6pm (Thu until 8pm). Closed major holidays. $9 (pay what you wish Thu 6pm–8pm). E or V train to 5th Ave.-53rd St.* Formerly the American Craft Museum, the institution changed its name in 2002. Since its founding in 1956, it has become a top venue for traditional and contemporary design. In 2008 the museum will move to Two Columbus Circle, tripling its exhibit space.

National Academy Museum★ – *1083 Fifth Ave. at E. 89th St. 212-369-4880. www.nationalacademy.org. Open year-round Wed & Thu noon–5pm, Fri–Sun 11am–6pm. Closed major holidays. $10. 4, 5 or 6 train to 86th St.* Though it may look rather modest from the outside, this 1902 town house contains 10,000 square feet of exhibit space. Here the museum displays rotating selections from its impressive, 5,000-piece collection of American art, which includes work by former National Academy of Art members Winslow Homer, John Singer Sargent and Jasper Johns.

Neue Galerie★ – *1048 Fifth Ave. at E. 86th St. 212-628-6200. www.neuegalerie.org. Open year-round Thu–Mon 11am–6pm (Fri until 9pm). Closed Tue–Thu & major holidays. $15. 4, 5 or 6 train to 86th St.* This Museum Mile newcomer was founded by cosmetics mogul Ronald Lauder in 2001 to display early-20C Austrian and German art. Mrs. Cornelius Vanderbilt III's Beaux-Arts mansion provides a  sumptuous backdrop for paintings by Gustav Klimt, Wassily Kandinsky and Paul Klee, as well as decorative arts by Bauhaus heavyweights Mies van der Rohe and Marcel Breuer.

Cafe Sabarsky

1048 Fifth Ave., lobby of Neue Galerie. Open Mon & Wed 9am–6pm; Thu–Sun 9am–9pm. 212-288-0665. Linzertorte, anyone? Named after Galerie cofounder Serge Sabarsky, this popular cafe is a culinary destination even when the galleries are closed, offering excellent tortes and strudels, smooth Viennese coffee, and Austro-Viennese staples like goulash and herring sandwiches. The setting was designed to re-create the heady atmosphere of early-20C Viennese coffeehouses, and it succeeds, especially when the piano player is in the house *(Wed–Thu 2pm–5pm, Fri 6pm–9pm).*

Studio Museum in Harlem★ – *144 W. 125th St., between Seventh & Lenox Aves. 212-864-4500. www.studiomuseum.org. Open year-round Sun & Wed–Fri noon–6pm, Sat 10am–6pm. Closed Mon, Tue & major holidays. $7. 2 or 3 train to 125th St.* Established in 1968 to provide studio space for African-American artists, this museum has since grown into a major visual art and performance center. In addition to temporary shows, a rotating selection of works from the 1,600-piece permanent collection is always on view in the recently expanded galleries. Check the calendar for special events.

Museum of Sex – *233 Fifth Ave. at 27th St. 212-689-6337. www.museumofsex. com. Open year-round daily 11am–6:30pm (Sat until 8pm). Closed Thanksgiving Day & Dec 25. $14.50.* Birds do it, bees do it. So why not have a museum about it? Past exhibits have traced the evolution of pornographic movies, and the origins of the pin-up girl from Victorian times. Many items on display are plucked from the permanent collection, including erotic films, books, posters and toys.

New York tends to look toward the future, not the past. But history is key to understanding this booming metropolis. The following sites offer glimpses of the Big Apple when it was just a tiny fruit.

City Hall★★

In City Hall Park, bounded by Broadway, Park Row, Lafayette & Chambers Sts. Visit by guided tour only (see sidebar). R or W train to City Hall.

New York's second official city hall, inaugurated in 1812, was designed by Joseph F. Mangin and John McComb Jr., who shared a prize of $350 for their efforts. Atop the graceful cupola is *Justice* with her scales; out front stands a statue of patriot Nathan Hale, who famously said, "I only regret that I have but one life to lose for my country" before being hanged by the British in 1776. Abraham Lincoln's body lay in state here in April 1865; 120,000 New Yorkers paid their respects. City Hall was half brownstone, not by design but by political penny-pinching, until 1956. Today it hosts welcoming ceremonies for visiting dignitaries and is the end point of ticker-tape parades.

> **Visiting City Hall**
>
> City Hall is only open to the public by the free, one-hour guided tours held Wednesday at noon, departing from Heritage Tourism Center at the south end of City Hall Park (Broadway at Barclay).

Interior Highlights — The gallery is ringed by Corinthian columns, which support a coffered dome pierced by a small circular window. The Governor's Room holds a desk used by George Washington.

City Hall Park★★— The publicly accessible corner of the park, cupped by Park Row and Broadway, sports benches, a spiffy fountain, and gas lamps.

South Street Seaport★★

Bounded by Water and John Sts., the East River and Peck Slip. 212-748-8600. www.south streetseaportmuseum.org. Free to wander; $8 to visit ships and museum (see sidebar). 2, 3, 4 5, J, M or Z train to Fulton St.

This waterfront historic district and shopping hub ranks as New York's third largest tourist attraction. Indeed, for some it might be too touristy—on warm days its pleasant cobblestone streets and wide-plank wharves are packed with sightseers, peddlers, and street performers.

But that's only half the picture. Spread throughout the district are half a dozen first-rate historical sites maintained by the **South Street Seaport Museum★★**, including maritime art galleries, a fleet of 19C vessels, and an old-fashioned print shop. During the summer, open-air concerts draw throngs of visitors to the piers.

Schermerhorn Row Galleries★★ – *12 Fulton St. between Front & South Sts.* Built between 1811 and 1813 as countinghouses and warehouses, these handsome brick structures now hold the South Street Seaport Museum's formidable collection of maritime arts and artifacts, including paintings, delicate scrimshaw (whalebone carvings), and ivory, lacquer and silk souvenirs from the China trade.

Pier 17 Pavilion★ – You'll find more than 100 shops and restaurants inside this three-story glass and steel structure, which offers excellent views.

Street of Ships★ – Board and explore the barque, square-rigger and lightship that are moored along Piers 15 and 16.

Bowne & Co. Stationers – *211 Water St. between Fulton & Beekman Sts. Open Fri–Tue 10am–5pm. Museum ticket not required.* At this charming 19C print shop, which still turns out wedding invitations and book plates, you can help make a Walt Whitman book on a treadle-operated press dating from 1901.

Harbor Cruises – Sail New York Harbor aboard the 1885 schooner *Pioneer*. Sponsored by the South Street Seaport Museum, cruises depart from Pier 16 *(May–Sept; 2hrs round-trip; advance reservations recommended; 212-748-8786).*

World Trade Center Site★★

Bounded by Church, Liberty, West & Barclay Sts. www.lowermanhattan.info and www.renewnyc.com. E train to World Trade Center; N or R train to Cortlandt St.
The world's largest commercial complex stood here from 1970 until the morning of September 11, 2001, when two hijacked planes were flown into the Twin Towers, killing 2,979 people and bringing the 110-story structures—

in which 50,000 people had worked—to the ground. It was the deadliest terrorist attack in US history. Rescue and recovery efforts began immediately, but there were few survivors of what *New Yorker* writer Hendrik Hertzberg called "the catastrophe that turned the foot of Manhattan into the mouth of hell." Eight buildings in all were destroyed. Workers carted off 1.5 million tons of steel and debris until the site was clear in May 2002, well ahead of schedule.

Rebuilding the site has proved far more difficult, thanks to the vast size of the project, the vast sums of money involved, and the number of parties with strong and often conflicting visions of its future.

Master Plan – Ultimately, the site will encompass an assortment of office buildings, memorials, parks and cultural venues, arranged according to a master plan created by Polish-born architect Daniel Libeskind and a revised design released by the Lower Manhattan Development Corporation. The centerpiece of the design is a 1,776 ft high-rise dubbed the Freedom Tower, surrounded by a cluster of shorter, angular glass office buildings. The two "footprints" of the original World Trade Center towers will be preserved as reflecting pools.

Castle Clinton National Monument★

Battery Park. 212-344-7220. www.nps.gov/cacl. Open year-round daily 8am–5pm. Closed Dec 25. 4 or 5 train to Bowling Green; 1 train to South Ferry.

This old fort has had nine lives. Well, at least five. It was completed in 1811 on an artificial harbor island created to protect Manhattan from possible attack during the War of 1812. That attack never happened, so in 1823 the fort was deeded to New York City and leased out as a restaurant and concert

Promenade★★

Meandering from Castle Clinton to the Staten Island Ferry Terminal, this walkway offers magnificent views of the bay, including the Statue of Liberty, Ellis Island and Governors Island.

hall called Castle Garden. French general Lafayette was feted here in 1824, and in 1850 "Swedish nightingale" Jenny Lind made her American debut on its stage, courtesy of circus ringleader P.T. Barnum. In 1855 the fort was returned to state hands and was opened as an immigrant landing depot. The

harbor between the castle and the shoreline was filled in and turned into a park in 1870. After a 50-year stint as the home of the New York Aquarium (now at Coney Island), Castle Clinton, with its 8 ft thick walls and gun ports, was designated a national monument in 1950. It's now best known as the place where you buy tickets for the Statue of Liberty ferry, though the National Park Service maintains a visitor center here and conducts tours throughout the day.

Federal Hall National Memorial★

[K] *refers to map on inside front cover. 26 Wall St. 212-825-6888. www.nps.gov/feha. Open year-round Mon–Fri 9am–5pm. Closed weekends & major holidays. J, Z or 2, 3, 4 or 5 train to Wall St.*

Federal Hall marks the spot of two historic firsts. New York's first city hall was opened here in 1702. Then in 1789, Federal Hall hosted the swearing-in of George Washington as the nation's first president. Alas, that structure was demolished in 1812 and sold as salvage for $425, but its 1842 replacement is sufficiently grand (and Greek) to recall the democratic ideals of the Founding Fathers. A towering bronze likeness of Washington stands outside on a plat-form if you need reminding. The recently remodeled interior is distinguished by its splendid central rotunda rimmed with balconies.

General Grant National Memorial★

Riverside Dr. at W. 122nd St. 212-666-1640. www.nps.gov/gegr. Open year-round daily 9am–5pm. Closed Jan 1, Thanksgiving Day & Dec 25. 1 train to 116th St.

Who's buried in Grant's tomb? The question that stumped 1950s game-show contestants continues to perplex visitors to his final resting place, a towering Neoclassical monument on a quiet bluff overlooking the Hudson River. A West Point graduate, Ulysses S. Grant (1822–85) made his name as Commander of the Union Army during the Civil War, then served two terms in the White House. "Let us have peace," he wrote to the Republican Party in 1868 when he decided to run for president under its auspices. These words are now engraved above the portico of this white-granite mausoleum, which contains the remains of Grant and his wife, Julia, as well as a small museum. But who's actually *buried* in Grant's tomb? No one—he and Julia lie in an above-ground crypt. Introductory talks *(on the hour)* help explain the history of the memorial and provide access to the crypt.

Morris-Jumel Mansion★

W. 160th St. & Edgecombe Ave. 212-923-8008. www.morrisjumel.org. Open year-round Wed–Sun 10am–4pm. $4. Closed Mon, Tue & major holidays. C train to 163rd St.

This hilltop mansion has stories to tell. Built for British colonel Roger Morris in 1765 as a summer retreat, the house today is Manhattan's oldest residence, containing a wealth of fine antiques and architectural details. A year after Morris abandoned the house in 1775, because his Loyalist sentiments were no longer appreciated in the colonies, George Washington commandeered it during the Battle of Harlem Heights. In 1810 it was acquired by French wine merchant Stephen Jumel, who preferred Napoleonic social circles to New York Society (the bed in the house was a gift from French Emperor Napoleon, who was a friend of the Jumels).

Theodore Roosevelt Birthplace National Historic Site★

28 E. 20th St. 212-260-1616. www.nps.gov/thrb. Open year-round Tue–Sat 9am–5pm. Period rooms may be visited by guided tour (40min) only; tours are held on the hour 10am–4pm, except noon. First-floor galleries may be viewed anytime. $3. Closed Sun, Mon & major holidays. 6 train to 23rd St.

A born-and-bred New Yorker, Theodore Roosevelt (1858–1919) was not your average city kid. As a sickly child, he was encouraged to exercise. The advice stuck, and the outdoors would become Roosevelt's lifelong passion. After going to college at Harvard, he worked as a rancher in the Dakota Territory, served as a colonel in the Rough Riders, hunted, collected specimens, and authored some 30 books. This in addition to being the 26th president of the United States (1901–09) and the winner of the Nobel Peace Prize in 1906.

Although Roosevelt's true birthplace was demolished in 1916, this Victorian brownstone was constructed and furnished to look as it did after his death.

Quick Bites

Teddy Roosevelt's old neighborhood, Gramercy Park, is now well known for its gourmet vittles. For lunch or an afternoon snack, try **71 Irving Place Coffee and Tea Bar** *(71 Irving Pl. between E. 18th & 19th Sts.; 212-995-5252)*, a friendly, garden-level cafe that serves up homemade quiche, waffles, sandwiches and soups, as well as some of the city's best coffee. Or whisk away to India via the tea room at **Tamarind** *(41–43 E. 22nd St.; 212-674-7400)* where you can sample exotic teas, pastries and sandwiches and other light Indian fare.

Villard Houses (New York Palace Hotel)★

[J] *refers to map on inside front cover. 451–457 Madison Ave. at E. 50th St. E or V train to Fifth Ave./53rd St.*

In 1881 Henry Villard, a Bavarian immigrant who founded the *New York Evening Post* and the Northern Pacific Railroad, hired the esteemed architectural firm McKim, Mead and White to design a group of six town houses—one for himself and the other five for sale. Inspired by a 15C Italian palazzo, the architects set six four-story structures around a U-shaped courtyard. Villard moved in with his family in 1883 but declared bankruptcy shortly afterward and had to sell the complex. It passed from private hands to the New York Archdiocese (St. Patrick's Cathedral is directly across the street) and then, in the 1970s, to Harry Helmsley, a developer who wanted to tear down the houses to build a hotel. The Landmarks Preservation Commission stopped him, so he built a 55-story skyscraper directly on top of the houses instead. The good news is that, as long as you don't look up, the houses appear much as they did when they were built, and some of the sumptuous interiors are preserved.

Interior – To get a sense of the grandeur of the original homes, enter the courtyard fronting Madison Avenue and step inside the central mansion, now the lobby of the posh New York Palace Hotel.

Urban Center – The Municipal Art Society, a feisty local preservation group since 1893, shares the north wing of the Villard Houses with several other nonprofit organizations. Here you'll find the Urban Center Bookstore *(see sidebar, below)* as well as free public galleries *(open Mon–Wed & Fri–Sat 10am–6pm, Sun 11am–5pm)* with rotating exhibits on architecture and design. You might also want to drop in to pick up a schedule of the Society's walking tours, which are widely considered the most in-depth and engaging in the city.

Urban Center Books

457 Madison Ave. 212-935-3595. www.urbancenterbooks.org. This friendly little bookstore on the first floor of the Villard Houses has 9,000 titles on architecture, urbanism and design. The shop was founded by the nonprofit Municipal Art Society in 1980 in an effort to foster a more informed discussion of architecture and the design arts in New York City—a goal no doubt informed by the decision to balance a skyscraper on the Villard Houses' heads.

Fraunces Tavern

54 Pearl St. 212-425-1778. www.frauncestavernmuseum.org. Open year-round Mon–Sat noon–5pm. $4. Closed major holidays. R or W train to Whitehall St.

With its slate roof and cream-colored portico, this handsome brick house gives visitors a sense of New York City as it might have appeared during the American Revolution. In 1719, Etienne de Lancey, who later gave his family name to Delancey Street, built a home here. Samuel Fraunces bought it in 1762 and turned it into a tavern. For ten days in 1783, Fraunces Tavern served as George Washington's last residence as general of the Patriot army, and on December 4 of that year he bade

farewell to his troops here before returning to his estate at Mount Vernon.

The building you see is only partly original; much of it was reconstructed in the early 20C. Today the ground floor is used as a bar/restaurant, and the upper floors display early-American decorative arts in period rooms.

Stone Street Historic District

Just steps away from Fraunces Tavern, Stone Street is one of the Financial District's most charming thoroughfares. On warm days its cobblestone expanse is festooned with the umbrella tables of restaurants and pubs. On cool and rainy days these spots provide a cozy respite from the concrete jungle. Try an espresso and a madeleine at the cheerful **Financier** patisserie *(no. 62; 212-344-5600; www.financierpastries.com)*. For pub grub and pints, try **Ulysses' Bar** *(no. 58; 212-482-0400; www.ulyssesbarnyc.com)*, serving lobster every Monday night and "cobblestone brunch" Sundays from 11:00am to 4:00pm.

New York Stock Exchange

[L] refers to map on inside front cover. 8–18 Broad St. at Wall St. www.nyse.com. 2, 3, 4 or 5 train to Wall St. The stock exchange has been closed to visitors since Sept. 11, 2001.

The New York Stock Exchange occupies a stunning eight-story Greek Revival building, home to the "Big Board" of nearly 3,000 publicly traded companies with a global market value of $20 trillion. Its beginnings however, were a bit more humble: The exchange was formally established on May 17, 1792, when 24 brokers met under a buttonwood (sycamore) tree outside the entrance at 20 Wall Street. Today, the classical facade hides one of the most technically sophisticated financial operations on the globe.

Trading Places

- On an average day, 1.46 billion shares, valued at $67 billion, are traded on the NYSE.
- NYSE is the world's largest stock exchange.
- The trading area of the NYSE is two-thirds the size of a football field.
- NYSE can process 4,000 orders, quotes and cancels per second.

HISTORIC CHURCHES

Cathedral of St. John the Divine★★

Amsterdam Ave at W. 112th St. 212-316-7540.
www.stjohndivine.org. Open daily 9am–6pm.
1 train to 110th St./Cathedral Pkwy.

This massive stone edifice, the seat of the
Episcopal Diocese of New York, is reputedly
the largest Gothic cathedral in the world.
Strangely though, it is only two-thirds
complete, and there are currently no plans to
finish it. The design incorporates a **Great Rose
Window** (it contains 10,000 pieces of glass)
overlooking the 601-foot-long nave.

Saint Patrick's Cathedral★★

[N] *refers to map on inside front cover. Fifth Ave.*
between 50th & 51st Sts. 212-753-2261.
www.saintpatrickscathedral.org. Open daily 6:30am–
8:45pm. B, D, F or V train to 47th–50th Sts./
Rockefeller Center.

Saint Patrick's may be the largest Roman Cath-
olic church in the US, but it looks practically
quaint amid the skyscrapers of Midtown. When
construction began in 1853, people complained that the cathedral was too far
out in the country. By the time it was completed in 1879—15 years later than
expected—the neighborhood was a fashionable residential quarter. Designed
by James Renwick, the cathedral is dedicated to the patron saint of the Irish.
The centerpiece of the interior is a 57-foot-high bronze canopy, or baldachin.

St. Paul's Chapel★★

Broadway between Fulton & Vesey Sts. 212-233-4164. www.stpaulschapel.org.
Open Mon–Sat 10am–6pm; Sun 9am–4pm. A or C train to Broadway-Nassau St.

Directly across the street from the World Trade Center site amid a grassy
fenced-in yard stands this picturesque chapel, which belongs to the Trinity
Church Parish *(below)*. Completed in 1766, the chapel is the oldest public
building in continuous use in Manhattan. George Washington worshiped here
regularly after his inauguration; today the chapel contains memorabilia from
the rescue efforts following September 11, 2001.

Trinity Church★★

74 Trinity Pl., at Broadway & Wall St. 212-602-0800. www.trinitywallstreet.org.
Open daily 7am–6pm. Guided tours daily 2pm. 2, 3, 4 or 5 train to Wall Street.

No match for the high rises of the Financial District today, this lovely Episcopal
church, with its 280 ft spire, was the tallest building in New York when it was
completed in 1846. The green, shady churchyard is dotted with old tomb-
stones; the most famous marks the grave of former Treasury secretary
Alexander Hamilton.

Parks

Far from being a concrete jungle, New York City has plenty of green space— if you know where to look. From the tiny vest-pocket parks sprinkled throughout the Village to the 843-acre Central Park, they come in all shapes in sizes. Some offer bike rentals, hot dog vendors and paddleboats; others just provide a quiet place to read a book. Take your pick: there are 1,700 to choose from. Here are some of the best.

Central Park★★★

Bounded by 59th & 125th Sts. and Central Park West & Fifth Ave. www.centralparknyc.org. N, R or W train to Fifth Ave.-59th St.; A, B, C, D or 1 train to 59th St./Columbus Circle.

Manhattan's playground is justifiably one of the most famous urban parks in the world. Not only is it massive—2.5 miles long and half a mile across—but it is rich and varied, offering a multitude of views; tons of recreational activities; and plenty of room to stroll, skate, cycle or just explore. Amazingly, it is totally man-made. In 1844 newspaper editor William Cullen Bryant urged the city government to acquire a "waste land, ugly and repulsive" north of 42nd Street (the city's northern border at the time) for use as a park. The city complied, buying what was then a swamp inhabited by squatters who raised pigs and goats. Calvert Vaux and Frederick Law Olmsted's naturalistic design was selected, and in 1858 clearing began. Some 3,000 mostly Irish workers and 400 horses moved an estimated billion cubic feet of earth over a period of 19 years to make the blueprint green.

In the northern part, rocky crags and dense thickets of trees were made to resemble the landscape of the Adirondack Mountains; in the south are more pastoral sections of rolling meadows, winding paths and delicate bridges. Today stately rows of skyscrapers and apartment buildings encircle the park, but Olmsted's vision remains stunningly intact.

Tavern On The Green

West side of the park at 67th St. 212-873-3200. www.tavernonthe green.com. The famed tavern is a perfect Sunday brunch spot, with stained-glass windows and glittering crystal chandeliers. Weather permitting, head for the outdoor cafe and bar, which is a dazzling sea of white lights and glowing lanterns at night.

Best of Central Park

For the **Carousel**, **Central Park Wildlife Center** *and* **Swedish Cottage Marionette Theatre**, *see Musts for Kids.*

Belvedere Castle – *At 79th St.* Calvert Vaux built this fanciful structure in 1872. It is home to a charming nature observatory, which has hands-on exhibits about the city's flora and fauna.

Bethesda Terrace – *At 72nd St.* This lovely sandstone plaza resembles a Spanish courtyard with its arcaded bridge, sweeping stairs and central fountain. It adjoins the Mall, a wide allée lined with handsome elms and sculptures depicting famous writers.

> **Touring Tip**
>
> Central Park's main visitor center is located in the Dairy, a whimsical 1871 structure just west of the Children's Zoo at 65th Street. Here you'll find maps, guides, history books and souvenirs, as well as information about the day's special events and activities *(call for seasonal hours).* The Central Park Conservancy's website *(212-310-6600; www.centralparknyc.org)* is also an excellent resource. In-line and ice skates *(in season)* may be rented at the Wollman Rink *(212-439-6900)*; rent boats and bicycles at Loeb Boathouse *(212-517-2233).*

Lake – *Between 71st & 78th Sts.* For a bit of old-fashioned fun, row a boat or hire a gondola to take you across this 22-acre expanse of water, or simply enjoy the view from the Loeb Boathouse, an acclaimed restaurant and cafe on the east side of the park between 74th and 75th streets.

Shakespeare Garden – The rustic four-acre garden on the rocky hillside between Belvedere Castle and the Swedish Cottage is scattered with plaques bearing quotations from the Bard.

Strawberry Fields – *West side at 72nd St.* Artist Yoko Ono contributed to the restoration of this 2.5-acre, teardrop-shaped garden honoring her husband, the late Beatle John Lennon, who was murdered nearby in 1980.

Bryant Park★★

W. 42nd St. at Sixth Ave. www.bryantpark.org.
B, D, F, V or 7 train to 42nd St.-Bryant Park.

With its delicate green folding chairs, pebble walkways and London plane trees, this gracious formal park behind the New York Public Library is Midtown's only large green space. Designated public land since the late 17C, in 1853 and 1854 the site hosted New York's first world's fair. Thirty years later it was named for the poet and activist William Cullen Bryant. If you happen to notice more than the usual number of laptop users here, it's because the whole park was outfitted with free wireless Internet access in 2002. Other perks include free outdoor movies on Monday nights in summer, and concerts.
Check the website or call 212-512-5700 for a schedule.

Battery Park★

Bordered by Battery Pl. & State St. 4 or 5 train to Bowling Green;
1 train to South Ferry.

On the southwestern tip of Manhattan, the maze of stone and steel monoliths dominating the Financial District suddenly gives way to a 21-acre expanse of greenery whose twisting paths are lined with vendors, street performers and artists selling their wares. Running along the harbor, the park's **promenade★★** offers stellar views of the Statue of Liberty.

Things To See In Battery Park

Statue of Liberty★★★ – Ferries to the world-famous monument and to the **Ellis Island Immigration Museum★★** leave from Battery Park. *See Landmarks and Museums chapters.*

Castle Clinton National Monument★ – Formerly West Battery, this round fort stood offshore until 1870, when the land in between it and the Financial District was filled in. It contains the Statue of Liberty ticket office as well as a National Park Service visitor center. *See Historic Sites.*

Sphere★★ – Near the north entrance of the park, at the intersection of Battery Place and State Street, is one of the most moving artifacts of September 11, 2001—a 15-foot-diameter, 22-ton brass ball by Fritz Koenig that once glittered in the World Trade Center's vast plaza. Salvaged from the rubble, the sphere now resembles a battered suit of armor. It stands beside an eternal flame.

Union Square★

Bounded by E. 14th & E. 17th Sts. and Park Ave. & University Pl. 4, 5, 6, L, N, R, Q or W train to 14th St./Union Square.

The greenery is mostly kept out of reach behind wrought-iron fences, but walks and benches beneath a thick canopy of trees make the park a pleasant place to stroll or rest. At the tiered plaza at the southern end, street performers strut their stuff and political activists stage vigils and protests, a tradition that goes back to the early 20C, when several radical organizations had offices in the area. Andy Warhol established his pop-cultural "Factory" in the ornate Decker Building (1893) at 33 Union Square West in the early 1960s; it has since been converted into condos and a wine store.

Union Square Greenmarket★

E. 17th to E. 14th Sts., between Park Ave. & University Pl. www.cenyc.org. From 8am to 6pm on Monday, Wednesday, Friday and Saturday, Upstate New York's farm bounty comes to this bustling market—a favorite of chefs city-wide. Arrive early for the best selection of tubers and herbs, fresh poultry and eggs, fresh flower arrangements, and wonderful pastries and breads.

Washington Square★

At the south end of Fifth Ave., at the intersection with Waverly Pl.
Any train to W. 4th St.-Washington Square Park.

This lively square at the heart of Greenwich Village teems with students, skateboarders, dog-walkers, chess players and other locals at all hours of the day and night. Originally a marshland and a favorite hunting ground of the early colonists, the site became a potter's field in the 18C (about 1,000 skeletons were unearthed during renovations in the 1960s). Following its transformation into a park in 1826, it spurred the growth of a fashionable residential enclave of redbrick town houses, including the well-preserved row on Washington Square North. Henry James's novel, *Washington Square*, written in 1881, was set in a house that once stood at no. 18.

Washington Arch★

Designed by Stanford White in 1891, this white marble Village landmark was built to memorialize George Washington's inauguration as the first US president. The arch measures 30 feet across and 77 feet high; gracing the sides are two sculptures of Washington, one as a soldier, the other as a civilian.

New York is a lively place in part because it is a city of neighborhoods, each with its own character, yet always in flux. From block to block, you never know what you'll come upon. Walking is the best way to find out; that's why so many visitors leave New York complaining about sore legs.

Chinatown★★

The heart of the district is bounded by Canal, Worth & Baxter Sts. and the Bowery. A staffed visitor information booth (open year-round Sun–Fri 10am–6pm, Sat 10am–7pm) is located in the triangle formed by Canal, Walker & Baxter Sts. www.explorechinatown.com. N, Q, R, W, 6, J, M or Z train to Canal St. See map, opposite.

Sprawling Chinatown is a veritable city within a city. The narrow streets are lined with colorful shops stocking everything from lychee to lipstick, while storefront restaurants serve up all manner of Asian cuisine. The first Chinese to settle in New York were men who came via the western states, where they had worked in the California goldfields or on the transcontinental railroad. The majority had no intention of staying; they merely wished to make their fortunes and return to comfortable lives in China. Ultimately though, many formed families or were joined by relatives from back home. Today Chinatown is one of New York's most densely populated neighborhoods, and it continues to grow past its old boundaries into Little Italy and the formerly Jewish Lower East Side. Crowded on weekends, the area bursts its seams at **Chinese New Year** (first full moon after January 19), when dragons dance in the streets accompanied by banner-carrying attendants and fireworks.

Shopping – Mulberry and Mott streets are lined with shops piled high with displays of bamboo plants, tea sets, silk dresses, Chinese lanterns, fans and the like. Canal Street between Broadway and Mulberry Street is world-famous for being crammed full of tiny stalls selling knock-off designer goods, especially handbags and scarves.

Neighborhoods

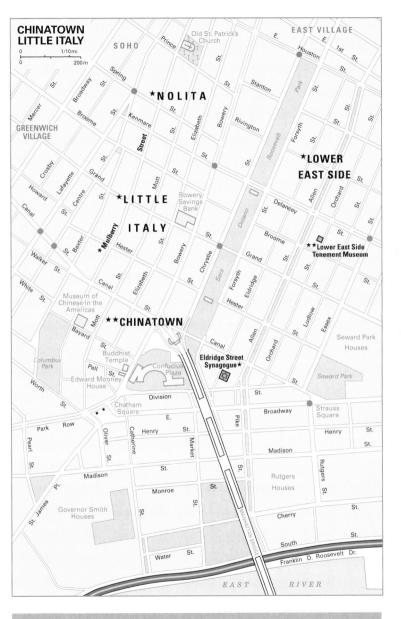

Dim Sum

A visit to Chinatown just isn't complete without a visit to one of its renowned dim sum palaces. Among your best bets is **Vegetarian Dim Sum House** at 24 Pell Street *(212-577-7176)*, which serves meat-free versions of the standards. For gourmet dim sum, try **Dim Sum Go Go** *(5 E. Broadway; see Must Eat)*.

Gallery Hopping in Chelsea★

Chelsea's many galleries are concentrated between 20th and 30th streets west of Tenth Avenue. Three not to miss: **Matthew Marks** (523 W. 24th St.; 212-243-0200; www.matthewmarks.com); **Gagosian** (555 W. 24th St.; 212-741-1111; www.gagosian.com); and **Gladstone Gallery** (515 W. 24th St.; 212-206-9300; www.gladstonegallery.com). For a list of shows and opening receptions, as well as a map, pick up a free **Gallery Guide** at any major gallery.

Chelsea★★

West of Sixth Ave., between W. 14th & W. 30th Sts.
1, C or E train to 23rd St.; M23 bus to Tenth Ave.
See map on inside front cover.

Beautifully refurbished brownstones and a thriving arts scene have made Chelsea a very desirable address in recent years, especially in the gay community. It was named after the London neighborhood in the mid-18C, but most of its housing stock dates to the 19C, when the quarter was laid out. Today Chelsea is *the* place in New York for gallery hopping.

Rubin Museum of Art★★ and **Chelsea Art Museum★** – See Museums.

Chelsea Historic District★ – W. 20th, 21st & 22nd Sts., between Ninth & Tenth Aves. Here stand some of Chelsea's loveliest brownstones. Note especially the Greek Revival **Cushman Row** (406–418 W. 20th St.), dating from 1840.

Greenwich Village★★

Bounded by Houston & W. 14th Sts., between Broadway and the Hudson River.
A, B, C, D, E, F or V train to W. 4th St.; 1 train to Christopher St. See map, opposite.

New York's historic bohemia centers on Washington Square (see Parks) and extends west to the Hudson in a beguiling tangle of streets lined with trees and town houses. Started as an Algonquin Indian settlement called *Sapokanikan*, the site gave rise to a British village in 1696. Artists and intellectuals, including Edgar Allan Poe, began arriving in the 1840s. The trickle turned into a flood in the early 1900s, and the 1960s saw figures such as Bob Dylan putting down roots here. Since then the struggling-artist crowd has moved to the edgier East Village, but Greenwich Village retains a charm all its own.

Bleecker Street★★ – A stroll up Bleecker Street will show you the full range of Village life. The intersection of Bleecker and MacDougal Streets is the epicenter of New York University's student district. Venture northwest (the street runs at an angle to Manhattan's grid) and you'll find a profusion of Italian bakeries and delis between Sixth and Seventh avenues. Keep going, and you'll enter the quaintest part of the village. Most of the row houses here were built between 1820 and 1855. End your stroll at **Magnolia Bakery** (no. 401; 212-462-2572) and sample of one of their thickly frosted cupcakes, which enjoy a cult following.

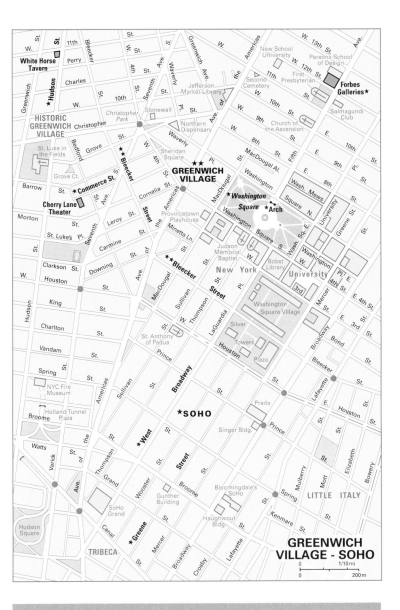

TriBeCa★

1 train to Franklin St. www.tribeca.org. Far less crowded and commercial than its neighbor SoHo, the wedge-shaped district named for its shape and location (TRIangle BElow CAnal) is an intriguing district of warehouses, art spaces, luxury co-ops, and chic restaurants such as **Chanterelle** *(2 Harrison St.)*, **Nobu** *(15 Hudson St.)* and Robert De Niro's **Tribeca Grill** *(375 Greenwich St.).*

Upper East Side★★

From E. 59th St. to E. 97th St., between Central Park & the East River.
N, R or W train to Fifth Ave. See map on inside front cover.

Although Millionaires' Row—Fifth Avenue—is now Museum Mile, the Upper East Side is still the wealthiest neighborhood in the city. In the late 19C, rich industrialists including Andrew Carnegie and Henry Clay Frick began building mansions on the large lots along Fifth Avenue, abutting the park. The ladies who lunch followed on their heels, moving into then-new luxury apartment buildings along Park Avenue and town houses on the side streets.

Fifth Avenue★★★ — You'll find more cultural capital on this strip than on virtually any street in the world. Three not to miss: the **Frick Collection★★★** *(at E. 70th St.)*, the **Metropolitan Museum of Art★★★** *(at E. 82nd St.)* and the **Guggenheim Museum★★** *(at E. 88th St.). See Museums.*

Madison Avenue★★ — *See Must Shop.* Chock-a-block with exclusive boutiques, Madison Avenue is also home to the **Whitney Museum★★** *(at E. 75th St.; see Museums)* and the **Carlyle Hotel★** *(at E. 76th St.; see Nightlife),* famous for its cabaret acts.

Upper West Side★★

From Columbus Circle to W. 125th St., between Central Park and the Hudson River.
Any train to Columbus Circle/59th St. See map on inside front cover.

The Upper West Side remains an enclave of literate liberals and performing artists drawn to the area's world-famous cultural venues, parks and tidy brownstones. Development has been relatively recent. In the late 19C, much of the area was still populated by stray goats. When New York's first luxury apartment house was erected on West 72nd Street and Central Park West in 1884, it was considered so far away from the heart of the city that it was dubbed the **Dakota** (Henry Hardenbergh's Gothic pile has since become famous as the site of John Lennon's murder). Noel Coward, Babe Ruth, Dustin Hoffman, and Jerry Seinfeld are just some of the famous residents who have called this neighborhood home over the years.

Upper West Side Highlights

- **American Museum of Natural History**★★★ – *Central Park West between W. 77nd & W. 81st Sts. See Museums.*

- **New-York Historical Society**★★ – *2 W. 77th St. at Central Park West. See Museums.*

- **Cathedral of St. John the Divine**★★ – *Amsterdam Ave. at W. 112th St. See Landmarks*

- **Lincoln Center**★★ – *Broadway between W. 62nd & W. 66th Sts. See Performing Arts.*

Harlem★

Bounded by 110th & 135th Sts. between Madison Ave. & Frederick Douglass Blvd. (Eighth Ave.). A staffed visitor information booth is located at 163 W. 125th St. at Adam Clayton Powell Jr. Blvd. (Seventh Ave.). A, B, C, D, 2 or 3 train to 125th St. See map on inside front cover.

Though only a fraction of the city's African Americans live in Harlem anymore, the neighborhood continues to nurture its history as a fulcrum of black culture. The neighborhood dates back to 1658 but was mostly rural until the railroad and elevated trains linked it to the rest of the city in the 19C. By the early 1890s, it was one of New York's most fashionable enclaves. The Harlem Renaissance came in the 1920s when black musicians (Count Basie, Duke Ellington) and writers (Zora Neale Hurston, Langston Hughes) electrified the world with their originality. Recent investment has brought new life into this quarter. Former president Bill Clinton, for instance, established his offices on 125th Street, and the famous **Apollo Theater***(see Performing Arts)* just completed a $12 million face lift.

Schomburg Center for Research in Black Culture★ – *515 Malcolm X Blvd./ Lenox Ave. (at W. 135th St.). Exhibition hall open year-round Tue–Fri noon–6pm, Sat 10am–6pm. Closed major holidays. 212-491-2200. www.schomburg center.org.* This branch of the New York Public Library system contains one of the world's largest archives relating to black heritage and mounts excellent temporary exhibits on African American history.

Studio Museum in Harlem★ – *144 W. 125th St. See Museums.*

Touring Tip

Because Harlem is so large, we recommend taking a tour. **Harlem Spirituals, Inc.** *(reservations required; 212-391-0900; www.harlemspirituals.com)* offers an evening visit of Harlem that includes soul food and jazz; a Sunday visit with a gospel and soul-food brunch; and a Wednesday-morning visit of Harlem with gospel. The **Municipal Art Society** also conducts walking and bus tours of the neighborhood on an occasional basis, as well as private tours by appointment *(212-935-3960; www.mas.org).*

Little Italy★

Bounded by Canal, Houston and Lafayette Sts. & the Bowery.
N, Q, R, W, 6, J, M or Z train to Canal St. See map p 65.

Little Italy is one of the tastiest corners of the city, with cafes for cappuccino and cannoli; grocery stores full of fresh pasta, salamis, olives and cheeses; and friendly and inexpensive red-sauce joints. The area took on its Italian character between the 1880s and the 1920s, when thousands of migrants left epidemics and poverty in Sicily and southern Italy, to come to the US. Mostly arriving through Ellis Island, they formed one of the city's tightest-knit communities. Though today the neighborhood is being pinched by Chinatown to the east and SoHo to the west, a sense of place still prevails.

Mulberry Street★ – Sometimes called the Via San Gennaro, Mulberry Street is Little Italy's main drag. It becomes a vast alfresco restaurant during the popular **Feast of San Gennaro** in mid-September, and is closed to traffic on weekends between May and October.

Nolita★ – This newly trendy area stretches from Broome to Houston streets on Mulberry, Mott and Elizabeth streets. Part of Little Italy, it was named by real-estate developers who in the 1990s wanted to distinguish it from the old neighborhood. The tactic worked. Today Nolita is bursting with cafes and boutiques, relatively few of which are Italian in character.

Best of Little Italy

Tile floors, tin ceilings, and ice-cream parlor chairs make **Caffe Roma** *(385 Broome St. at Mulberry St.; 212-226-8413)* one of the most appealing of Little Italy's cafes. Grab an outdoor seat to watch the world flow past. For a festive dinner, try the cheap-but-good **La Mela** *(167 Mulberry St., between Broome & Grand Sts.; 212-431-9493)*, a sprawling landmark that's open every night past midnight. Tucked around the corner from bustling Mulberry Street, **Ferrara** *(195 Grand St., between Mott & Mulberry Sts.; 212-226-6150)* is *the* place for cannoli, tiramisu, and Italian pastry. It's all made on the premises. If you're hungry at lunch, head to **Alleva Dairy** *(188 Grand St. at Mulberry St.; 212-226-7990)* and order a prosciutto, mozzarella, and roasted-pepper sandwich, the deli's specialty. Established in 1905, **Lombardi's** *(32 Spring St., between Mott & Mulberry Sts.; 212-941-7994)* dishes up thin-crust pies baked in coal-fired ovens and served on checkered tablecloths. Expect a wait on weekend nights.

Lower East Side★

Bounded by Houston, Canal and Clinton Sts. and the Bowery.
Visitor center: 261 Broome St., between Orchard & Allen Sts.
(open daily 9am–5pm; 212-226-9010; www.lowereastsideny.
com). F train to Delancey St.; B or D train to Grand St.
See map p 65.

Despite being one of New York's hippest 'hoods,' the
Lower East Side has, for the most part, a refreshing
lack of attitude and an astounding amount of local
pride. "Come one, come all" has been its message
to visitors since the 1880s, when it became the quintessential American melting pot. Though today's
immigrants tend to be young artists, history lives on
at the **Lower East Side Tenement Museum★★**
(see Museums) and in the neighborhood's many famous ethnic eateries.

Eldridge Street Synagogue★ – *12 Eldridge St., between Canal & Division Sts.*
Open year-round Sun, Tue–Thu 11am–4pm. Closed Jewish & national holidays.
Guided tours (call for times & prices). 212-219-0888. www.eldridgestreet.org.
Completed in 1887, Eldridge Street was the first synagogue built by Eastern
European Jews. The building, which is undergoing extensive renovation, boasts
a striking rose window set against an ornate Moorish facade.

A Nosher's Paradise

The Lower East Side was the original nosher's paradise, and for those in the know, it
remains so. Since opening in 1914, **Russ & Daughters** *(179 E. Houston St.; 212-475-4880)*
has been winning awards for its Caspian Sea caviar. For a tart accompaniment, go to
Guss' Lower East Side Pickles *(85 Orchard St.; 917-701-4000)*, founded in 1910. Need
your sugar fix? Stop in at **Sweet Life** *(63 Hester St.; 212-598-0092)*, the Lower East
Side's preeminent candy shop since 1982.

SoHo★

Bounded by Sullivan, West Houston, Lafayette & Canal Sts.
R or W train to Prince St, or C or E train to Spring St. See map p 67.

Home to dozens of artists and galleries in the 1980s, SoHo—short for South
of Houston (pronounced HOW-stun)—has more recently become one of New
York's most popular shopping districts. Visitors throng the neighborhood on
weekends, making even walking down the sidewalk difficult—especially given
the profusion of sidewalk tables piled with purses and jewelry, sunglasses,
scarves and the like. Weekdays are slightly more manageable. Though most of
its art galleries have decamped for Chelsea, some excellent ones remain. Two
to keep in mind are the **Drawing Center** *(35 & 40 Wooster St.)*, which cham-
pions drawings both historical and contemporary, and **Deitch Projects** *(76
Grand St.)*, which sponsors playful avant-garde mixed-media exhibits and
performances.

Don't be fooled by its cosmopolitan air—New York City loves to kid around. A city of parents, it teems with fun activities for families. Here's a roundup of some of our favorites.

American Museum of Natural History★★★

Central Park West between 77th & 81st Sts. 212-769-5200. www.amnh.org. Open year-round daily 10am–5:45pm. $15 adults, $8.50 children. Closed Thanksgiving Day & Dec 25. B or C train to 81st St. or 1 or 9 train to 79th St.

There's plenty of awesome stuff here to keep kids mesmerized for hours. Dinosaurs are a good place to start. Check out the huge barosaurus skeleton in the entrance rotunda, then ogle hundreds of specimens in six dazzling **fossil halls★★** on the fourth floor—the museum has the largest collection of verte-brate fossils in the world. Then proceed to the adjoining **Rose Center for Earth and Space★★**. Exhibits on the blue planet and its place in the universe are high-tech marvels, as are the space shows, which take place every half-hour in the Hayden Sphere: tip back in your comfy chair and let Tom Hanks or Harrison Ford be your guide *(advance tickets: 212-769-5200).* *For more kid-friendly activities at the museum, go to www.amnh.org/kids.*

Bronx Zoo★★★

Bronx River Pkwy. at Fordham Rd.. 718-367-1010. www.bronxzoo.com. Open Apr–Oct Mon–Fri, 10am–5pm; Sat–Sun 10am–5:30pm; $14 adults, $10 children (ages 3-12). Rest of the year daily 10am–4:30pm. 2 train to West Farms Sq./E. Tremont Ave.; an express bus ($4; exact change required) runs up Madison Avenue (see zoo website).

The country's largest urban zoo is set in a woodland park that's so pretty you might forget that just around the corner you could meet a giraffe or an ostrich. From elegant ibex to goofy gibbons, the animals here enjoy homes that mirror their natural habitats as much as possible, thanks to the Wildlife Conservation Society, which runs the place. The **Tiger Mountain★★** exhibit lets you see eye to eye with these Siberian cats. A **Children's Zoo★** *($3)* houses more than 500 animals and lets kids climb a rope spider web, try on a turtle's shell and feed goats, chickens and other barnyard critters.

Central Park★★★ for Kids

Bounded by 59th St & 110th St., Central Park West & Fifth Ave. 212-310-6600. www.centralparknyc.org. N, R or W train to Fifth Ave.-59th St.; A, B, C, D or 1 train to 59th St./Columbus Circle.

Besides offering plenty of space for sports and strolls, Central Park has attractions that appeal to kids of all ages. For more information on visiting the park, including details on boat and bicycle rental and ice skating, see the *Parks* chapter; for the day's calendar of events, drop by the visitor center in the Dairy, just south of the carousel *(call for seasonal hours; 212-794-6564).*

Carousel – *Midpark at 65th St. 212-879-0244. www.centralparkcarousel.com. Open Apr–Oct daily 10am–6pm (weekends 7pm). Rest of the year weekends only, 10am–dusk.* This 1908 carousel incorporates 58 hand-carved, hand-painted horses—some life size! Taking it for a whirl is a New York tradition.

Central Park Wildlife Center – *East side between 63rd and 66th Sts. 212-439-6500. Open Apr–Oct Mon–Fri 10am–5pm; weekends 10am–5:30pm. Rest of the year daily 10am–4:30pm. $8 adults, $3 children 3–12.* Animals in this 5.5-acre zoo have space to roam in natural settings. Among the biggest (literally) crowd pleasers are the frisky sea lions, which are fed at 11:30am, 2pm and 4pm. Kids can pet and feed goats, sheep and a Vietnamese pot-bellied pig at the **Tisch Children's Zoo**, which is especially popular with the stroller set.

Belvedere Castle – *Midpark at 79th St. 212-772-0210. Open year-round Tue–Sun 10am–5pm. Closed major holidays.* The Henry Luce Nature Observatory features kid-friendly hands-on exhibits about the city's flora and fauna.

Swedish Cottage Marionette Theatre – *W. 79th St. and West Dr. 212-988-9093. Shows Tue–Fri 10:30am & noon, Sat–Sun 1pm. $6 adults, $5 children. Reservations required.* Original puppet shows, many drawn from fairy tales, are staged daily at this charming 1877 Swedish schoolhouse.

Empire State Building★★★

Fifth Ave. & 34th St. 212-736-3100. www.esbnyc.com. Open year-round daily 8am–2am (last elevator up at 1:15am). $19 adults, $17 ages 12-17, $13 ages 6-11. Any train to 34th St-Herald Square. See Landmarks.

Kids love a trip to the top of this 102-story Art Deco landmark, where they can get dizzying views of New York City and its neighboring states. High-speed elevators zip up to the 86th floor, which has both a glass-enclosed area and spacious outdoor promenades on all four sides of the building. High-powered binoculars let you zoom in close on your favorite sites.

Statue of Liberty★★★

Liberty Island. 212-363-3200. www.nps.gov/stli. Closed Dec 25. For visit information, see Landmarks.

A trip to New York wouldn't be complete without getting up close and personal with Lady Liberty, the towering symbol of democracy in New York harbor. Though the winding corkscrew staircase to the crown has been closed, you can still go inside the statue on one of two guided tours. (Be sure to reserve a spot in advance!) Both tours bring you through the museum exhibits, but the observatory tour is especially fun, since it allows you access to the 10th-floor observation platform, which boasts awesome views.

Family Fun in the Big Apple

For more tips on what to do with kids—from suggested itineraries to parents' testimonials—go to New York City's official tourist website *(www.nycvisit.com)*, and type "kids" into any search box.

Lower East Side Tenement Museum★★

97 Orchard St. at Broome St. 212-431-0233. www.tenement.org. Visitor center and gift shop open Mon–Fri 11am–6pm (Mon until 5:30pm); Sat & Sun 10:45am–6pm. Tenement may be visited by 1hr guided tour only. F train to Delancey St.

Kids ages five and older—especially ones from the country or the suburbs—will never forget a visit to one of the cramped tenement apartments at 97 Orchard Street, especially if Victoria Confino is their guide. This turn-of-the-20C teenager, played by a sassy young actress, will show you her apartment and relate in witty detail how work was parceled out, how marriages were arranged and how much monthly rent her family paid for the tiny space—$15, including coal *(tours Tue–Fri every 40 minutes 1:20–5pm; Sat–Sun every 30 minutes 11:15am–4:45pm. $17 adults, $13 students; advance tickets: 866-811-4111 or through the website).*

Sony Wonder Technology Lab★

[C] *refers to map on inside front cover. In the Sony Plaza Building, 550 Madison Ave. at E. 56th St. 212-833-8100. www.sonywondertechlab.com. Open year-round Tue–Sat 10am–5pm, Sun noon–5pm. Closed Mon & major holidays. E or V train to Fifth Ave./53rd St.*

Interactive exhibits at this futuristic play space in Sony Plaza will dazzle even the most tech-savvy kid. Parents take note: If this is one of your child's must-sees, reserve at least a week ahead.

Children's Museum of Manhattan

212 W. 83rd St. (between Broadway & Amsterdam Ave.). 212-721-1234. www.cmom.org. Open Tue–Sun 10am–5pm. Closed Mon & major holidays. $8 (adults & children). 1 train to 79th St.

Kids can spend many happy hours at Manhattan's only museum geared for children. Five floors of hands-on exhibits explore the environment, forensic science and much more.

New York Aquarium★★

W. 8th St. & Surf Ave., Brooklyn. 718-265-3474. www.nyaquarium.com. Open Jun–Aug Mon–Fri 10am–6pm (weekend closing at 7pm). Rest of the year closing times vary. $12 adults, $8 children (ages 2-12). F or Q train to W. 8th St.

Just off the Coney Island boardwalk, this world-renowned aquarium—it's run by the Wildlife Conservation Society—shows off 8,000 slippery critters in naturalistic indoor and outdoor habitats. Kids can explore the world of jellies in the **Alien Stingers★★** exhibit and view octopi, walrus, sea lions, seahorses and penguins in the underwater viewing galleries of **Sea Cliffs★** *(for more information, see Boroughs/Brooklyn).*

Coney Island

Brooklyn. www.coneyislandusa.com. Open in summer, week-ends in fall and spring. D, F, N or Q train to Stillwell Ave.

New York's beachfront amusement park is a little seedy but tons of fun. Take a stomach-dropping ride on the **Cyclone**, a 1927 wood-framed roller coaster, ride the gigantic Ferris wheel or catch a circus side-show. A stroll along the wood-plank boardwalk that skirts the beach is a Coney Island tradition, as is a Coney Island hot dog from **Nathan's Famous** *(1310 Surf Ave. at Stillwell Ave.).*

Intrepid Sea, Air & Space Museum

Pier 86 (W. 46th St. at Twelfth Ave.). 212-245-0072. www.intrepidmuseum.org. Currently undergoing renovation in Staten Island; scheduled reopening late 2008.

Berthed at a pier in the Hudson River, the 1943 aircraft carrier USS *Intrepid* measures 898 feet and weighs in at 42,000 tons. The carrier was a veritable city, providing its 3,500-member crew with everything from a haircut to an ice-cream sundae.

Must Go: Performing Arts

You can hardly think of New York City without thinking of Broadway shows, Off-Broadway shows, and Off-Off Broadway shows. As the undisputed arts capital of the US, New York offers entertainment for nearly every taste and budget. Here's a list of some of the most popular options in the city, but it's by no means comprehensive. *For daily schedules and critics' picks, consult the publications listed in Practical Information.*

Broadway★★

The Broadway Line: 888-276-2392. www.livebroadway.com.

They say the neon lights are bright on Broadway—and rightly so. "The Great White Way" is synonymous with the country's best and most popular theater productions. Of course, this street isn't the only one lined with theaters; it merely forms the spine of the **Theater District★**, which extends roughly between 40th and 53rd streets from Sixth to Eighth avenues. Crowd-pleasing musicals abound, with some of the best hoofers burning up the boards and bringing down the house in shows like *The Lion King*, *Chicago*, and *The Producers*. Movie stars and pop-music legends will often open shows that run for years with rotating casts—some better than the originals.

TKTS

Waiting until the last minute doesn't always mean paying top dollar when it comes to theater tickets. If you're flexible with what you want to see, you can save 25 to 50 percent on tickets at TKTS. You can buy tickets for same-day evening performances and matinees at the **Times Square booth** *(Broadway & W. 47th St.; tickets for 2pm matinees go on sale at 10am; tickets for 8pm shows go on sale at 3pm)* or at the **South Street Seaport booth** *(corner of John & Front Sts.; tickets for evening shows go on sale at 11am; matinee tickets available a day in advance)*. Digital signs at both locations indicate which shows have tickets; availability changes hourly. For the best selection, arrive early, though sometimes tickets are released just before the 8pm curtain *(cash & traveler's checks only)*. For more information, check online at www.tdf.org/tkts.

Lincoln Center★★

Columbus Ave. between W. 62nd & W. 66th Sts. 212-546-2656. www.lincolncenter.org.

Devoted to drama, music and dance, Lincoln Center for the Performing Arts is a 16-acre complex comprising five major theater and concert buildings, a library, a band shell and two outdoor plazas. Visually, the space is stunning, with sleek rectangular buildings of glass and Italian travertine marble arranged around a central fountain. The centerpiece is the **Metropolitan Opera House**, with its 10-story colonnade. Although guided tours are available daily, the best way to appreciate

**92nd Street Y:
The Other Side of the Park**

1395 Lexington Ave. at E. 92nd St. 212-415-5500. www.92y.org. Founded in 1874 as the Young Men's Hebrew Association, this Y has grown into one of the city's best-loved cultural centers. The 92nd Street Y presents world-class concerts of classical, folk and cabaret music, lyric theater and jazz, and readings by eminent authors.

Lincoln Center is to attend a performance. The regular season lasts from September through May; the summer season is filled with festivals and special events, including Lincoln Center Out of Doors, Midsummer Night Swing, Mostly Mozart, and the Lincoln Center Festival.

Resident Companies

Chamber Music Society of Lincoln Center – *212-875-5788. www.chambermusicsociety.org; performing at alternate sites in 2007–2008; call for information.* The nation's premier chamber music ensemble performs in 1,100-seat Alice Tully Hall.

Jazz at Lincoln Center – *212-875-5350 (tours), 212-721-6500 (tickets). www.jalc. org.* Under the direction of Wynton Marsalis, the Lincoln Center Jazz Orchestra performs at the Time Warner Center at Columbus Circle *(Broadway & W. 60th St.)*. Three spaces here are dedicated to jazz: the 1,100-seat Frederick P. Rose Hall, the 400-seat Allen Room, and the 140-seat Dizzy's Club Coca-Cola.

Metropolitan Opera – *212-362-6000. www.metopera.org.* The world-renowned company presides in the 3,788-seat Metropolitan Opera House.

New York City Ballet – *212-870-5570. www.nycballet.com.* The troupe performs in the 2,792-seat New York State Theater, designed by Philip Johnson.

New York City Opera – *212-870-5570. www.nycopera.com.* The New York City Opera also performs in the New York State Theater.

New York Philharmonic – *212-875-5656. www.newyorkphilharmonic.org.* New York's resident symphony performs in 2,742-seat Avery Fisher Hall.

The Rockettes

...5-6-7-8. The world's finest precision dance team began as the Missouri Rockettes in St. Louis in 1925, and they've been the star attraction at Radio City Music Hall since opening night—December 27, 1932. Today the annual Radio City Christmas Spectacular, with its cast of 140 leggy dancers, is a dazzling New York holiday tradition *(early Nov– late Dec; 2–5 performances daily)*.

Radio City Music Hall★★

[P] *refers to map on inside front cover. 1260 Sixth Ave. at W. 50th St. 212-247-4777. www.radiocity.com.*

A treasured New York landmark, this Art Deco performance palace is a spectacular place to see a show— particularly the resident Rockettes, whose kick-line spectaculars are as mesmerizing as the place itself. Radio City opened its doors in 1932 and began by presenting the best vaudeville acts and silent pictures of its day. The 5,882-seat theater has been the site of some fantastic live performances (everyone from Frank Sinatra to Björk has graced its stage) as well as the annual Tony Awards for live theater. Its proscenium arch rises six stories.

• **State-of-the-art stage** allows musicians in the orchestra and organists at the two electric Wurlitzers to be whisked away behind the walls or below the floor during performances—without missing a note!

Brooklyn Academy of Music★

30 Lafayette Ave., Brooklyn. 718-636-4100. www.bam.org.

Widely regarded as New York's premier venue for avant-garde performance, Brooklyn Academy of Music (BAM) hosts live music, dance and theater in two historic buildings. The elegant 1,100-seat opera house has hosted everyone from Enrico Caruso to Laurie Anderson. The 900-seat Harvey Theater is home to the Brooklyn Philharmonic Orchestra and is a favorite venue for cutting-edge theater troupes from around the world. BAM's annual **Next Wave Festival** *(Oct–Dec)* is one of the liveliest peforming-arts festivals in the city.

Carnegie Hall

156 W. 57th St. at Seventh Ave. 212-247-7800. www.carnegiehall.org.

With its fine acoustics, majestic Carnegie Hall is one of the world's most prestigious concert venues. Named after steel magnate Andrew Carnegie, the Italian Renaissance structure opened in 1891 with Tchaikovsky's American conducting debut. Since then its stage has hosted luminaries from Gustav Mahler to Bob Dylan. Carnegie Hall has three performance spaces—the main 2,804-seat auditorium; the 268-seat **Weill Recital Hall**, which resembles a Belle Epoque salon; and the high-tech **Zankel Hall**, with 599 seats—and a museum.

Apollo Theater

253 W. 125th St. 212-531-5305.
www.apollotheater.com.

This world-famous Harlem theater has
been a hotbed of African-American
music and entertainment since 1934.
Every Wednesday night is Amateur
Night—"where stars are born and
legends are made." Who knows? You
might see the debut of the next Ella
Fitzgerald, James Brown, Michael
Jackson or Lauryn Hill—all of whom
launched their careers here. Tickets
($18–$40) can be purchased at the box office *(open Mon, Tue, Thu & Fri 10am–*
6pm, Wed 10am–8:30pm, Sat noon–6pm) or through Ticketmaster *(212-307-*
4100; www.ticketmaster.com).

City Center

131 W. 55th St between Sixth & Seventh Aves. 212-581-7907. www.nycitycenter.org.

After being threatened with demolition in the 1940s, this 1923 Shriner's temple
reopened as a concert hall with ticket prices topping out at $2. Since 1994, the
popular Encore Series has brought recognition to rarely heard works of
American musical theater. City Center's best-known resident companies are
the **Alvin Ailey American Dance Theater** *(www.alvinailey.org)* and the
American Ballet Theatre *(www.abt.org)*.

Off-Broadway Theater

www.offbroadwayonline.com.

There are 150 spaces across the city that qualify as
Off-Broadway theaters. While many of them lie
outside the Theater District, the designation indi-
cates more than their location. Off-Broadway tickets
cost less than those to Broadway shows. Theaters are
also smaller (100–499 seats), and performances more
intimate. Some shows, like Stomp and Blue Man
Group, remain on Off-Broadway for years. Others
(The 25th Annual Putnam County Spelling Bee, Rent,
Proof, A Chorus Line) start Off-Broadway and move
to Broadway once they become bona fide hits.

Off-Off Broadway

If Off-Broadway
doesn't get you far
enough away from
the Great White Way,
consider going Off-
Off. Performances
can be hit or miss, but
the ticket price (usu-
ally less than $20)
justifies a little risk
taking. See the *Village
Voice* for reviews.

Famous Off-Broadway Companies & Theaters

The following venues are all are based downtown:
- **Public Theater** *(212-260-2400; www.publictheater.org)*
- **Atlantic Theater Company** *(212-645-1242; www.atlantictheater.org)*
- **New York Theater Workshop** *(212-460-5475; www.nytw.org)*

Don't get stressed if you can't see everything on your trip to New York. That's just what a New Yorker would do. Instead, try to relax and have fun, mixing up museum visits with simple pleasures. Here are some places to start.

Staten Island Ferry★

212-639-9675 (311 within New York). www.siferry.com. Year-round daily 24hrs/day roughly every 30min (hourly midnight-6am). R or W train to Whitehall St.; 1 train to South Ferry.

For quick (25 minutes each way) but dazzling views of the Statue of Liberty and New York Harbor, hop aboard the blissfully free Staten Island Ferry—it's the best sightseeing deal in town *(see Boroughs/Staten Island)*.

Times Square★★

Seventh Ave. & Broadway between W. 42nd & W. 46th Sts. Any train to Times Sq.-42nd St.

Packed with people day and night (night is a relative term, as it never goes dark here), Times Square is the blazing heart of New York; a sensory burst of gigantic neon advertisements and electronic tickers, Jumbotrons, traffic, crowds and vendors. The newly renovated (some say sanitized) district stretches along Broadway and Seventh Avenue between 42nd and 46th streets and overflows into the side streets, which host dozens of Broadway theaters *(see Performing Arts)*. Times Square is especially festive at night, when after-theater audiences pour out into the streets to enjoy its bright lights and carnivalesque atmosphere. Don't expect to find any "old" New York here—with its

Times Square Information Center

Overwhelmed? You can get all your questions answered—and much more—at this helpful visitor center, ensconced in the Art Deco lobby of the landmark Embassy Movie Theatre *(Seventh Ave. between W. 46th & 47th Sts.)*. Open daily from 8am to 8pm, it contains a staffed information desk, plentiful brochures, several computer terminals with free Internet access, a U.S. Post Office, a Broadway ticketing service, public restrooms, and copies of free newspapers known for their cultural event listings, including the *Village Voice* and *The L Magazine*. The center's Website *(www.timessquarenyc.org)* is also chock-full of news and advice.

corporate logos and international crowds, the area is now more than ever the crossroads of the world. Among the most audacious newcomers:

• The **ESPN Zone** (1472 Broadway at W. 42nd St.) is not only a sports store but a massive arcade and sports bar with more that 200 TV screens.

• **Toys R Us** (1514 Broadway at W. 44th St.) is a toy store and a small amusement park, complete with an indoor Ferris wheel and an animatronic dinosaur.

• **Virgin Megastore** (1540 Broadway at W. 45th St.) claims to be the world's largest music/entertainment emporium, with 70,000 square feet of space.

Carriage Rides in Central Park

Carriages line up on Central Park South (59th St.) between Fifth & Sixth Aves. and at Tavern on the Green. 212-246-0520. $35–$100, depending on time of day & length of ride. N, R or W train to Fifth Ave.

Horse-drawn carriages have been a fixture in Central Park since the Victorian era. This old-fashioned mode of transport remains one of the most romantic and popular ways to see the southern tip of Central Park, even (or especially!) during the winter months, when drivers will give you a blanket to snuggle up in.

Circle Line Cruises

Pier 83 (W. 42nd St. at West Side Hwy.). 212-563-3200. www.circleline42.com.

Anchors aweigh! Taking a narrated boat ride is one of the best ways to learn about the city—Manhattan is an island, after all. And these guides know their stuff, peppering their running historical commentary with the latest in New York gossip (for instance, which celebrity paid how many millions for their apartment?). The full island tour takes three hours, and on a sunny day the time breezes by. But there are shorter tours, too. Look online or check at the ticket counter for options, schedules and prices—and keep in mind that a Circle Line cruise is included with a CityPass discount ticket booklet *(see p 10)*.

Grand Central on the Half Shell

Grand Central Terminal, lower level. 212-490-6650. www.oysterbarny.com. S, 4, 5, 6 or 7 train to Grand Central-42nd St.

Sure, its vaulted ceiling is magnificent (the tiles were designed by 19C artisan Rafael Gustavino), but the **Grand Central Oyster Bar** doesn't coast on atmosphere. New Yorkers come here for some of the best fresh seafood in the city. Settle in at the counter and order oysters Rockefeller and clam chowder—it's a tradition—or have a full meal in the restaurant. The steady flow of diners makes for great people-watching.

Starry Nights

On the first Friday of every month, the **American Museum of Natural History** features live jazz performances, tapas and wine inside the great glass cube that is the **Rose Center for Earth and Space** *(see Museums)*. Hour-long jazz sets take place at 6pm and 7:30pm.

Musts For Fun

Madame Tussaud's

234 W. 42nd St. between Seventh & Eighth Aves. 800-246-8872. www.nycwax.com.
Open daily 10am–8pm. $29. Any train to Times Square.

If a picture's worth a thousand words, then how many is a wax model worth?
Judge for yourself at this popular "museum," named after a woman who made
death masks from the guillotined heads of prominent victims of the French
Revolution. In this branch of the famous London museum you will find more
than 200 popular and historical personalities come eerily to life in galleries
that show them off, warts and all (when they say realistic, they mean it!).

Lights, Camera, Action!

You've seen them on TV—people just like you sitting in the studio audiences of your
favorite programs, hooting and hollering on cue. If that's what you're after, try to get
tickets to a taping. Though most tickets are spoken for months or even years in
advance, you may be able to get stand-by tickets if you're willing to call at a specific
time or wait in line. Here's how to get information about some of the shows:

Good Morning America – *212-580-5176 or www.abcnews.com.*

Late Night with Conan O'Brien – *212-664-3056 or www.nbc.com.*

The Late Show with David Letterman – *212-247-6497 or www.cbs.com.*

Live with Regis and Kelly – *www.bventertainment.go.com.*

Saturday Night Live – *212-664-3056 or www.nbc.com.*

If all else fails, you can jostle for a spot on camera outside the street-level Today
Show studio (30 Rockefeller Plaza between Fifth & Sixth Aves.; Mon–Fri 7am–10am;
www.nbc.com), or take a **guided tour of NBC studios** (see Skyscrapers/GE Building).

See a Game at Yankee Stadium★

161st St. & River Ave., the Bronx. Tours: 718-579-4531. Tour at ticket information at
www.yankees.com. B, D or 4 train to 161st St.-Yankee Stadium.

Catching a baseball game in "the House That Ruth Built" (so called for its
short right-field porch, built to maximize Babe Ruth's left-handed swing) is
the modern-day equivalent of watching a gladiatorial contest in the Roman
Coliseum. As the pin-striped players take the field with military precision,
the crowd explodes with hoots and hollers and, if the game is a good one,
continues in the same vein for hours—fueled by a steady diet of beer, hot
dogs and Cracker Jacks. If you're not around for the April-to-October season
or if games are sold out (they often are), take a stadium tour. This way you'll
get to to check out the dugout, the press box, the clubhouse and Monument
Park, where bronze plaques commemorate Yankee legends Lou Gehrig, Joe
DiMaggio, Mickey Mantle and others. The famous stadium will host its last
season in 2008. Beginning in 2009, the Bronx Bombers will move to a new
stadium being constructed to the north.

Serendipity 3

225 E. 60th St. between Second & Third Aves. 212-838-3531. www.serendipity3.com. Open Sun–Thu 11:30am–midnight (Fri until 1am; Sat until 2am). N, R, W, 4, 5 or 6 train to Lexington Ave.-59th St.

Visitors rarely come upon this kid-friendly general store/soda fountain/ restaurant serendipitously anymore. On the contrary: they flock to it, especially on weekend days, when it provides the perfect pre- or post-Bloomingdale's boost. The place was founded in 1954 as New York's first "coffeehouse boutique"; Andy Warhol declared it his favorite sweet shop and is said to have paid his bill here with drawings. Today frozen hot chocolate—served in parfait glasses, topped with fluffy whipped cream and sucked through a straw—is the speciality of the house. This patented delicacy, along with upscale diner fare, is served under an array of Tiffany lamps, amid a fascinating arrangement of historic bric-a-brac.

Seasonal New York

As the proverb goes, for everything there is a season, and that is certainly true in New York. Even if fall and spring offer the best chance of nice weather, summer and winter have lots of fun traditions as well. Here are a few.

Winter – Under the watchful gaze of *Prometheus*, caught stealing fire from the gods, is the center of a winter wonderland— **Rockefeller Center's sunken skating rink** *(212-332-7654)*. It's cozy— okay, tiny—but taking a turn on the ice in such a splendid setting is unforgettable. If you

need more room to execute your Hamill Camel, head uptown to Central Park's tree-framed **Wollman Rink**, near Columbus Circle *(212-439-6900; www.wollmanskatingrink.com)*. Skate rentals are available at both rinks.

Another holiday tradition: Check out the **window displays at Macy's** *(34th St. & Sixth Ave.)* and **Saks Fifth Avenue** *(Fifth Ave. & 49th St.)*. If you're at Saks, be sure to mosey across the street to see the nine-story **Christmas tree** ablaze with tiny lights in Rockefeller Plaza.

Summer – July and August can be hot and sticky, and many New Yorkers flee the city. Well, that's their prerogative, but they're missing out on a great civic tradition: **free performances**, offered by some of the Big Apple's most renowned theatrical troupes and music groups. The **Metropolitan Opera**, the **New York Philharmonic** and the **Public Theater** all offer freebies in New York's parks. **SummerStage** in Central Park hosts some terrific performers as well. *For more information, see Calendar of Events or check local listings.*

Must Shop

Fashion victims unite! No matter if you have champagne tastes and a beer budget, there's something to suit everyone in New York City. Consider taking a guided shopping tour, a popular way to hit the hotspots and get the inside scoop on bargains *(Shop Gotham; 212-209-3370; www.shopgotham.com).*

Fifth Avenue★★★

Upscale boutiques and department stores line world-famous Fifth Avenue between 34th and 59th streets. Even if you don't step foot inside a single one, their elaborate window displays turn a simple stroll into a dazzling adventure.

Fifth Avenue Roll Call

- **Bergdorf Goodman** – *Between 57th & 58th Sts. 212-753-7300. www.bergdorf goodman.com.* Understated elegance has been the key to the store's lasting appeal among the "ladies who lunch" and the men who love them.

- **Cartier** – *At 52nd St. 212-753-0111. www.cartier.com.* The French jewelry firm bought this Renaissance-style palazzo in 1917.

- **FAO Schwarz** – *At 58th St. 212-644-9400. www.faoschwartz.com.* Kids of all ages adore this world-famous toy store, founded German immigrant Frederick August Otto Schwarz in 1862.

- **Rockefeller Center** – *47th–51st Sts. 212-632-3975. www.rockefellercenter.com.* Purchase anything from books in Japanese to to Italian leather in the shops lining these plazas and underground concourses.

- **Saks Fifth Avenue** – *At 49th St. 212-753-4000. www.saks.com.* Upper floors at Saks' flagship feature upscale boutiques with plenty of clerks on call.

- **Tiffany & Co.** – *At 57th St. 212-755-8000. www.tiffany.com.* For silver, pearls and diamonds, Tiffany is still the *crème de la crème.*

Madison Avenue★★

Though it has stiff competition from Fifth Avenue, Madison Avenue between 59th and 78th streets remains, inch for inch, the most luxurious shopping strip in the city. Native son **Calvin Klein** anchors the southern end with a palace showcasing clothing and home furnishings *(no. 654; 212-292-9000; www.calvinklein.com).* **Barneys** *(no. 660; 212-826-8900; www.barneys.com)* has nine exuberant stories of ultrachic brand names. Impeccable French accessories designer **Hermès** has a shop at 691 Madison Ave. *(212-751-3181; www.hermes.com).* **Emilio Pucci** flogs wildly patterned togs at 24 E. 64th St. *(212-752-4777; www.emiliopucci.com).* **Emanuel Ungaro** has a pink staircase to match is signature floral print dresses *(no. 792; 212-249-4090; www.emanuelungaro.com).* Men gravitate toward **Giorgio Armani** for European-style suits and torso-hugging T-shirts *(no. 760; 212-988-9191; www.giorgioarmani.com).* Bronx-born **Ralph Lauren**—née Ralph Lifschitz—displays his timeless fashions in the opulent 1895 Gertrude Rhinelander Waldo House *(no. 867; 212-606-2100; www.polo.com).* Farther north you'll find the super-luxe French shoe store **Christian Louboutin** *(no. 941; 212-396-1884).* Japanese designer **Issey Miyake** showcases wearable art at no. 992 *(212-439-7822; www.isseymiyake.com).*

Times Square★★

42nd–46th Sts. & Broadway.

New York's commercial heart is ablaze day and night with stores and vendors vying for visitors' attention. Kids will love **Toys R Us** *(1514 Broadway; 800-869-7787; www.toysrus.com),* where they can greet Barbie in a life-size town house.

Bridgemarket★

E. 59th St. & First Ave.

An immense, cathedral-like hall under the roadway to the Queensboro Bridge has been restored to its original grandeur, thanks to the efforts of British designer Terence Conran, who in the early 1990s signed on to develop a shop and restaurant on the site. Credit for the glorious results goes largely to the father-and-son team Rafael and Rafael Guastavino, Italian artisans who covered the vaulted ceilings with thousands of clay tiles in the early 1900s.

Today the **Conran Shop** *(407 E. 59th St.; 866-755-9079; www.conranusa.com)* houseware and design emporium is a favorite among savvy shoppers.

Diamond and Jewelry Way

W. 47th St. between Fifth & Sixth Aves. www.diamonddistrict.org.

This 750 ft long block is home to nearly 90 per cent of the diamond wholesale trade in the US. Listen closely, and even on the sidewalk you may hear cut, carat, color and clarity—the four "C"s—discussed in a bewildering variety of languages. Most deals, however, are conducted inside these glittering emporia, either in upper-floor dealers' booths or in backrooms. Feel free to browse the heavily monitored showrooms.

Time Warner Center★

Broadway at Columbus Circle.

Cupping the west side of Columbus Circle with its vast semicircular facade, this huge complex (2004) contains 40 shops arranged around a four-story atrium. The most popular (among locals) is the gargantuan Whole Foods supermarket in the basement. Other stores include J. Crew clothing store, Godiva Chocolatier, Borders Books and Music, TUMI luggage, Dean & DeLuca, Eileen Fisher, and Davidoff jewelers. And don't miss the Time Warner Center's stellar lineup of celebrity chef-run restaurants, which includes Per Se (Thomas Keller), Masa (Masa Takayama), Porter House New York (Michael Lomonaco) and Café Gray (Gray Kunz).

Must Shop

Shopping Neighborhoods

Crystal District – In 2002 the city unveiled its newest shopping destination: a five-block stretch of Madison Avenue *(from 58th to 63rd Sts.)* that's now home to the world's richest concentration of crystal decorative objects and jewelry.

Nolita★ – *Mulberry, Mott, & Elizabeth Sts. between Broome & Houston Sts.* For shopaholics, the acronym for "North of Little Italy" has become synonymous with fashion daring and originality. In recent years, young designers fleeing the high rents of SoHo have turned Little Italy pizzerias and shoe-repair businesses into trendy boutiques. Come see for yourself what all the fuss is about.

SoHo★ – *Bounded by Canal, W. Houston, Sullivan & Lafayette Sts.* Try walking down SoHo's narrow sidewalks on a sunny Saturday and you'll see what this 26-block historic district is *really* famous for. High-end boutiques have brought in world-class architects to transform their storefronts into glittering show-

places—check out Rem Koolhaas's space-age dressing rooms inside **Prada** *(575 Broadway)*. Among the 100 other shops, you'll find Mac Cosmetics, DKNY, Helmut Lang, and Emporio Armani. Outside, vendors display jewelry and knock-off designer items.

Sample Sales

One of the best ways to get designer clothes at rock-bottom prices in New York is to attend a sample sale or a trunk sale. This is when designers unload everything that didn't make it into mass production. Elbows can be sharp, but the savings are fantastic. Check *New York Magazine* or *Time Out New York* for this week's sales.

The Sparkling Lineup *(addresses below are on Madison Ave.)*

Baccarat *(no. 625; 212-826-4100; www.baccarat.com)* traces its lineage back to 1764. Its 4,500-square-foot US flagship has two floors of sparkling wares.

Daum *(no. 694; 212-355-2060; www.daum.fr)* has been around for 120 years and showcases designs specially created by avant-garde artists, including Salvador Dalí.

Lalique *(no. 712; 212-355-6550; www.cristallalique.com)* offers crystal as well as luxury goods including silk scarves, perfume and porcelain.

Steuben *(no. 667; 212-752-1441; www.steuben.com)* moved to this location in May 2002, selling its trademark animal figurines as well as bowls and vases.

Swarovski *(no. 625; 212-308-1710; www.swarovski.com)*, a family-owned company based in Austria, is the world's leading manufacturer of full-cut crystal.

More Stores

Macy's★ – *151 W. 34th St., between Broadway & Seventh Ave. 212-695-4400. www.macys.com.* The world's largest department store holds 2.1 million square feet of space and more than 500,000 different items. The store's so big that it even has a visitor center *(34th St. balcony)* with information about where to find what. Foreign visitors can pick up a 11-percent discount card here.

Bloomingdale's – *1000 Third Ave., between E. 59th & 60th Sts. 212-705-2000. www.bloomingdales.com.* "Bloomie's," as it's affectionately called, has been an Upper East Side shopping mecca for decades. Here, high fashion applies not only to clothes but to all the merchandise, from bonbons to shower curtains.

Century 21 – *22 Cortlandt St., between Broadway & Church Sts. 212-227-9092. www.c21stores.com.* You won't find the gracious service or orderly displays here that you'll find at the Fifth Avenue department stores. But if it's name-brand bargains you're after, you've come to the right place. A New York institution.

Zabar's – *2245 Broadway at W. 80th St. 212-787-2000. www.zabars.com.* No ordinary grocery store, Zabar's is world renowned for its selection of gourmet treats. Though it started as a Jewish deli, it now stretches a city block and sells unusual foods from around the globe, including more than 600 varieties of imported cheeses. Dip inside for ready-to-eat chicken pot pie, Texas barbecue ribs and onion-crusted salmon fillets. Or bring home a chocolate babka for a friend. They'll love you for it.

Outdoor Shopping

Some of the city's best bargains and most unusual merchandise can be found in outdoor markets. For fresh food, nothing beats the city's farmer's markets. The **Union Square Greenmarket★** is the most popular *(see Parks),* but there are dozens of others sprinkled throughout the five boroughs *(schedule & information: 212-788-7476; www. cenyc.org).* New York's top antiques flea market is the **Annex/Hell's Kitchen Flea Market** *(W. 39th St., between Ninth & Tenth Aves.; 212-243-5343; www.hellskitchenflea market.com),* held year-round every Saturday and Sunday from sunrise to sunset.

Jump on the subway at three or four in the morning and you'll find the rumor is true: New York really *is* the city that never sleeps. Gotham comes alive each night in its pubs and clubs, many offering music and live entertainment. Here's a selection of some of the most atmospheric venues. Check local listings for what's on tap when you're in town.

CABARET

Cafe Carlyle – *35 E. 76th St. at Madison Ave. 212-744-1600. www.thecarlyle.com.* A timeless institution, the Carlyle was singer Bobby Short's home base for decades prior to his death in 2005. The mural-bedecked space now hosts world-famous musicians from saxophonist Woody Allen to gravelly voiced alto Elaine Stritch.

Joe's Pub – *425 Lafayette St. at Astor Pl. 212-539-8777. www.joespub.com.* Singer-songwriters the world over clamor to perform at this intimate downtown supper club, part of the Public Theater complex. Arrive early or make a dinner reservation to snag a good seat.

Oak Room – *59 W. 44th St. at Sixth Ave. 212-840-6800. www.thealgonquin.net.* Ensconced in the Algonquin Hotel, which lent its name (and its bar) to the acid-witted writers who became known as the Algonquin Roundtable, the cozy Oak Room serves up first-rate cabaret. Recent performers have included Andrea Marcovicci and John Pizzarelli.

COCKTAIL LOUNGES

Bemelmans Bar – *35 E. 76th St. at Madison Ave. 212-744-1600. www.thecarlyle.com.* The sister venue of Cafe Carlyle *(above)* recently got a makeover that deepened its Rat Pack-era allure. Cocoon-like banquettes make listening to jazz here a decadent experience.

Campbell Apartment – *15 Vanderbilt Ave., between E. 41st & E. 42nd Sts. 212-953-0409.* You can't help but be amazed when you enter this ornate vaulted space, which executive John W. Campbell turned into a sumptuous office in the 1930s. Today it's a one-of-a-kind bar that feels like a speakeasy—though it's just steps from bustling Grand Central Terminal. A hidden gem.

Lobby Lounge – *8 W. 60th St. at Broadway. 212-805-8800.* Not your ordinary hotel bar, the Lobby Lounge—perched on the 35th floor of the Mandarin Oriental Hotel in the Time Warner Center—has vertiginous views of Central Park South and the city beyond. Perfect for a nightcap or an afternoon tea.

Monkey Bar – *In the Hotel Elysée, 60 E. 54th St. (between Park & Madison Aves.). 212-838-2600. www.elyseehotel.com.* Try a sparkling monkey (champagne and Chambord) in this beautifully restored former haunt of author Tennessee Williams and actress Tallulah Bankhead.

Rainbow Grill – *30 Rockefeller Plaza. 212-632-5100. www.rainbowroom.com.* Few bars are more romantic than this one, an Art Deco lounge with panoramic views of Manhattan from the 65th floor. Come for a cocktail and stay for a Northern Italian dinner (jackets requested; no T-shirts, jeans or sneakers). On selected Fridays and Saturdays, the adjoining Rainbow Room hosts a live big band for a night of dinner and dancing.

COMEDY CLUBS

Gotham Comedy Club – *34 W. 22nd St., between Fifth & Sixth Aves. 212-367-9000. www.gothamcomedyclub.com.* One of New York's leading stand-up clubs, Gotham hosts everyone from unknowns to celebrities—as long as they're funny. You be the judge. Jerry Seinfeld has been known to drop in here to test-drive his new material.

Upright Citizens Brigade Theater – *307 W. 26th St. between Eighth and Ninth Aves. 212-366-9176. www.ucbtheatre.com.* Saturday Night Live-style sketch comedy and improv—sometimes even with SNL stars—are trotted out nightly here at bargain prices.

DANCE CLUBS

Club Shelter – *20 W. 39th St., between Fifth & Sixth Aves. 212-719-4479. www.clubshelter.com.* It may not be in the most happening 'hood, but this Saturday-night house party has offered some of the best, sweatiest beats in the city for fifteen years, a virtual eternity in the notoriously fickle club world.

Lotus – *409 W. 14th St., between Ninth and Tenth Aves. 212-243-4420. www. lotusnewyork.com. .* The quintessential Meatpacking District club, this three-tiered glamour palace boasts a fancy restaurant, multiple lounges and a disco.

S.O.B.'s (Sounds of Brazil) – *204 Varick St. at Houston St. 212-243-4940. www.sobs.com.* New York's premier world-music venue has a tropical décor, a cabana-like bar, and a menu with tasty Brazilian and Portuguese specialties. When the music starts pumping, the crowd hits the dance floor.

JAZZ

Blue Note Jazz Club – *131 W. 3rd St., between Sixth Ave. & MacDougal St. 212-475-8592. www.bluenote.net.* Incredible acoustics, an intimate setting and a stellar lineup (often two top artists in one evening) make this one of the city's best jazz clubs. Continental cuisine is served late.

Iridium Jazz Club – *1650 Broadway at W. 51st St. 212-582-2121. www.iridiumjazzclub.com.* This relative newcomer to New York's jazz scene has won fans with its impressive roster of artists and its 600-bottle wine list.

Jazz Standard – *116 E. 27th St., between Lexington & Park Aves. 212-576-2232. www.jazzstandard.net.* There's no minimum food or drink order here, because the owners are certain you'll want baby back ribs and pan-fried catfish from Blue Smoke restaurant upstairs. Superlative bookings and crystalline sound make this a great choice.

Lenox Lounge – *288 Lenox Ave., between 124th & 125th Sts. 212-427-0253. www.lenoxlounge.com.* When film producers search for an authentic Harlem club of the 1920s, they look no farther than the Lounge. Live jazz and blues are played six nights a week in the Zebra Room. Southern fried chicken, barbecued ribs, and crab cakes are served up daily.

Village Vanguard – *178 Seventh Ave. S. 212-255-4037. www.villagevanguard. com.* Photographs of Bill Evans and other jazz greats line the walls, and top-billing jazz musicians take the stage at New York's oldest jazz club, in Greenwich Village. Musicians often drop in after their gigs at other clubs for late-night jam sessions.

No Smoking

Since April 2003, almost all bars and clubs in New York have been made smoke-free by law. Exceptions include places that make more than 10 percent of their money through tobacco sales. If you want to light up indoors, try **Circa Tabac** *(32 Watts St.; 212-941-1781)*, where an efficient ventilation system keeps the fumes to a minimum.

ROCK AND POP

Beacon Theatre – *2124 Broadway at W. 74th St. 212-496-7070.* Come see touring singer-songwriters like Bob Dylan, Lenny Kravitz and Lucinda Williams at this wondrous 1929 venue, a stunning assemblage of rococo curlicues and red velvet that somehow manages to be vast and intimate at the same time.

Fillmore NY at Irving Plaza – *17 Irving Pl. at E. 15th St. 212-777-6800. www.irvingplaza.com.* Big indie bands like Built to Spill and the New York Dolls, as well as legends like Tom Jones and Deborah Harry, have played at this newly renovated club, now run by Live Nation; stand close to the stage for the best acoustics.

Knitting Factory – *74 Leonard St., between Broadway & Church St. 212-228-8490. www.knittingfactory.com.* Legendary home of the musical avant-garde, the club hosts live jazz and rock upstairs, more experimental music below—and 18 beers on tap.

Pianos – *158 Ludlow St. 212-505-3733.* Housed in a former piano shop, this wallet-friendly, starkly minimalist newcomer books an impressive lineup of DJs and garage-rock bands.

A trip to New York can sometimes feel as hectic as staying at home, but it doesn't have to be that way. Whether you're fighting jet lag or your feet are aching after days of pounding pavements, a visit to one of these spas can be just what the doctor ordered.

Acqua Beauty Bar

7 E. 14th St. 212-620-4329.
www.acquabeautybar.com.

Think you're already on vacation? Think again. Acqua Beauty Bar offers a range of "journeys" for the face, body and nails. Treatments range from high-tech facials (Medi-Lift, microdermabrasion) to an Indonesian Ritual of Beauty, complete with ground rice body scrubs and herbal masques. There's even an airbrushed Fantasy Tan for people who want a sun-kissed look without the wrinkles.

Ajune

1294 Third Ave., between E. 74th & 75th Sts. 212-628-0044. www.ajune.com.

Aestheticians at this Uptown oasis offer personalized treatments for the muscle-sore and wrinkle-weary. Low-tech solutions include the facial *du jour*, which draws on the curative powers of fresh fruits and essential oils; and the ginger massage, which uses moisture and heat to work out all that tension. For those wanting eternal youth—or at least the appearance of it—there are botox and collagen injections.

Bliss Spa

568 Broadway at Prince St., 2nd floor; 12 W. 57th St. between Fifth and Sixth Aves., 3rd floor; 541 Lexington Ave. at E. 49th St. 212-219-8970. www.blissworld.com.

Since opening its first tiny outpost in SoHo in 1996, Bliss has become one of New York's hottest spots for beautification and relaxation. The most popular facial is the Herbie, which combines a basic cleansing and exfoliation facial with a full-body rub-down and herbal wrap. The ultimate skin and massage treatment is the Ginger Rub. You'll be slathered in crushed ginger and essential oils, then wrapped in foil and left to steep on a bed of hot water. Afterward, melt into a comprehensive 100-minute massage. Ahhh.

Eden Day Spa

388 Broadway, between Walker & White Sts. 212-226-0515. www.edenspany.com.

Relaxation is the name of the game at this TriBeCa staple, where treatments are refreshingly straightfoward. If you're really feeling indulgent, try the Day Dream: five hours of loving attention to your muscles, nails, skin and face.

Elizabeth Arden Red Door Salon & Spa

691 Fifth Ave. at 54th St. 212-546-0200. www.reddoorspas.com.

The extensive menu of services at Elizabeth Arden's Fifth Avenue flagship spa has something for every appetite. If it's a cut you need, the stylists here are top notch. Botox treatment? A plastic surgeon is on hand to administer one. However, the most popular choices remain the most basic ones: manicures and pedicures, facials, makeovers and aromatherapy massages.

Graceful Services

1095 Second Ave. at 57th St. 212-593-9904. www.gracefulservices.com. Graceful Spa: 205 W. 14th St. at Seventh Ave., 2nd floor. 212-675-5145. www.gracefulspa.com.

For a body-tingling, mind-expanding massage at a great price, these sister spas can't be beat. Calling on ancient Chinese wisdom, therapists work to get your life energy, or "qi," moving with three different types of massage: Chinese, Swedish and shiatsu. The original Upper East Side location is more spartan than the newer, more luxurious Chelsea outpost, but both offer a full range of services.

John Allan's Club

46 E. 46th St., 212-922-0361; 95 Trinity Pl., 212-406-3000. www.johnallans.com.

The people at this admirably efficient outfit know how to deliver maximum pampering in a minimum amount of time. The "Full Service" treatment, administered simultaneously by at least two clinicians, includes a shoe shine, a shampoo, a hair cut, a scalp massage, a hot-towel facial, a manicure and a beverage, and clocks in at only 35 to 45 minutes. It's perfect for busy Wall Street execs, Madison Avenue ad men—and scruffy travelers.

La Prairie Spa

Ritz-Carlton Hotel, 50 Central Park South. 212-521-6135. www.ritzcarlton.com.

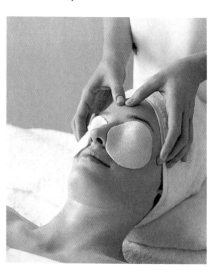

Can't slow down enough for a full treatment—consider one of La Prairie's Manhattan Minutes spa packages. Jet Lag Therapy includes aromatherapy massage, foot reflexology, and a facial. After-Shopping Paradise blends foot massage with a pedicure. For the one-hour Changing Room special, both you and your clothes get a good steaming, while you're treated to a manicure, a facial and a makeover.

Best of the Boroughs

Manhattan may be the heart of New York City, but a lot of life goes on in the four "outer" boroughs: the Bronx, Queens, Brooklyn and Staten Island, all of which were incorporated into the city in 1898. Here you'll find not only the vast majority of New Yorkers, but some of New York's best-loved—and least crowded—attractions.

THE BRONX

Home of the New York Yankees (aka "the Bronx Bombers"), the Bronx is New York's only borough located on the mainland. It was named after Jonas Bronck, a Swedish emigré who arrived here in June 1639. Today about half the borough's residents are Hispanic and 25 percent of its acreage is parkland.

Bronx Zoo★★★

Fordham Rd. at Bronx River Pkwy. 718-367-1010. www.wcs.org. Open Apr–Oct Mon–Fri, 10am–5pm, weekends & holidays until 5:30pm; $14 ($10 ages 3–12). Rest of the year open daily 10am–4:30pm. 2 train to E. Tremont Ave./W. Farm Sq.

It's a jungle out there—or at least it is at the country's largest urban zoo. Set in a 265-acre woodland park, the Bronx Zoo is so pretty you sometimes forget you're in the company of some of the most magnificent creatures on earth. From elegant ibex to goofy gibbons, the animals here enjoy homes that mirror their natural habitats as much as possible—the Wildlife Conservation Society makes sure of that. The zoo was founded in 1899. Today it showcases more than 4,000 animals and is an important center for researching and breeding endangered species.

Bronx Zoo Express

One of the easiest ways to get to the zoo is by bus. The MTA's BXM11 **express bus** *($5 each way; payable by exact change or MetroCard)* runs approximately every 20 minutes, picking up along Madison Ave. in Manhattan at 27th, 32nd, 39th, 47th, 54th, 63rd, 70th, 84th and 99th streets. The Bronx Zoo is the next stop after 99th Street.

Best of the Bronx Zoo

Skyfari★★ – Travel about the treetops from the zoo center to Wild Asia on this high-flying gondola. It's a quick and beautiful way to get across the park.

Tiger Mountain★★ – The zoo's spectacular tiger exhibit puts you just a whisker away from the largest member of the cat family. Meow!

Wild Asia★★ – The Bengali Express Monorail passes through 38 acres populated by free-roaming tigers, gaur cattle, red pandas and rhinoceroses.

Congo Gorilla Forest★★ – This 6.5-acre African rain forest counts more than 300 animals, including one of the largest breeding groups of lowland gorillas.

Children's Zoo★ – Here kids can feed domestic farmyard animals and see others in natural environments.

New York Botanical Garden★★

200th St. and Kazimiroff Blvd. 718-817-8700. www.nybg.org. Open Apr–Oct Tue–Sun 10am–6pm. Rest of the year Tue–Sun 10am–5pm. Closed Mon, Thanksgiving Day & Dec 25. $13 includes all gardens, tours and tram.
B, D or 4 train to Bedford Park Blvd., then the Bx 26 bus east to Moshulu Gate entrance.

Green thumbs won't want to miss this gorgeous horticultural landmark, located directly north of the Bronx Zoo. Founded in 1891, it is one of the largest and oldest gardens in the country. Numerous walking trails wind through its 250 acres past such favorites as the Rose Garden, the Rock Garden, the Native Plant Garden and the Daylily Collection. The site also features 50 acres of original forest. Peak season is late spring/early summer, though you'll see interesting exhibits and plenty of plants in bloom throughout the year.

Touring Tip

Take the Metro-North Harlem line from Grand Central Station to the Botanical Garden stop, directly outside the garden gate. The trip takes only 20 minutes!

Enid A. Haupt Conservatory★★ – Opened in 1902, this glorious Victorian structure showcases global plant communities from rain forests to deserts.

Everett Children's Adventure Garden★ – Forty hands-on exhibits allow kids and families to explore how plants live and function.

Wave Hill★

W. 249th St. & Independence Ave. 718-549-3200. www.wavehill.org. Open mid-Apr–mid-Oct Tue–Sun 9am–5:30pm (Wed until 9pm Jul & Aug); rest of the year Tue–Sun 9am–4:30pm. Closed Mon & major holidays. $6 (free Tue & Dec–Feb). You can take the subway and then transfer to a bus (see Wave Hill's Website for details), but we recommend taking the Metro-North Hudson Line commuter train from Grand Central Terminal to Riverdale (free shuttle bus meets northbound trains Apr–Oct weekends) or the BxM1 or BxM2 express buses from Midtown Manhattan to 252nd St. (see Bronx Zoo Express sidebar, opposite).

From its spectacular perch above the Hudson River, Wave Hill—a gardener's paradise—seems worlds away from the city. This enchanting 28-acre estate was built as a country home in the 1840s and has had some illustrious occupants, including Theodore Roosevelt's family and Mark Twain. Today 18 acres of its grounds have been landscaped into seven separate gardens, containing more than 3,000 species. Must-sees here include the herb garden, the alpine garden, the dry garden, the wild garden, the pergola and the conservatory.

Yankee Stadium★ *See Musts for Fun.*

BROOKLYN

New York's most populous borough occupies the western tip of Long Island. Founded by the Dutch in 1636, the area was named Breuckelen ("broken land") after a small town near Utrecht. The population exploded after the Brooklyn Bridge opened in 1883. Today Brooklyn is a mix of separate neighborhoods, from staid Brooklyn Heights to honky-tonk Coney Island to verdant Park Slope; the last a popular haven for young well-to-do families.

> ### Walking Tours
>
> For an insider's view of Brooklyn, the **Brooklyn Historical Society** *(128 Pierrepont St.; 718-222-4111; www.brooklynhistory.org)* does walking tours of the area. They also maintain the borough's only history museum.

Brooklyn Bridge★★★ *See Landmarks.*

Brooklyn Botanic Garden★★

900 Washington Ave. 718-623-7200. www.bbg.org. Open mid-Mar—Oct Tue—Fri 8am–6pm, weekends & holidays 10am–6pm. Rest of the year Tue–Fri 8am–4:30pm, weekends 10am–4:30pm. Closed Mon & major holidays. $8 (free Sat 10am–noon, all day Tue & weekdays mid-Nov–Feb). 2 or 3 train to Eastern Pkwy.; B, Q or S train to Prospect Park.

Bordering the east edge of Prospect Park and serving as a de facto backyard for the Brooklyn Museum of Art, this refreshing oasis covers 52 acres and includes one of the finest assemblages of roses in the country. Its outdoor gardens are separated into nine distinct styles, including a Shakespeare garden and a Japanese garden. The **Steinhardt Conservatory★** houses the country's largest bonsai collection.

Brooklyn Heights★★

If you decide to walk over the Brooklyn Bridge, consider taking a stroll around this lovely neighborhood at the other end. It's a wealthy enclave of narrow, tree-lined streets bordered with historic brownstones. Willow and Pierrepont streets are particularly picturesque. Montague Street is the commercial strip, with cafes and high-end boutiques. And don't miss the **esplanade**, which runs along the East River from Montague to Orange Street and affords magnificent views of the Financial District across the river.

Brooklyn Museum of Art★★

200 Eastern Pkwy. 718-638-5000. www.brooklynmuseum.org. Open year-round Wed–Fri 10am–5pm, weekends 11am–6pm. Closed Mon, Tue, Jan 1, Thanksgiving Day & Dec 25. $8. 2 or 3 train to Eastern Pkwy.

Best known for its Egyptian collection and its superb cache of American paintings, the Brooklyn Museum is the second-largest art museum in the US. It illustrates art history from ancient times to the present with selections from its 1.5-million-piece collection. The monumental Beaux-Arts structure, designed by McKim, Mead and White, was opened in 1897 but has been undergoing modifications throughout its existence. The latest round has brought some huge improvements. In 2003 viewing space for the Egyptian collection doubled, the Beaux-Arts Court displaying European painting was totally refurbished, and the museum opened a public study center for its collection of American art.

First Floor – **African art★★**, arts of the Americas and a sculpture garden.

Second Floor – Asian and Islamic art; Chinese jades and Persian carpets.

Third Floor – The stunning **Egyptian art collection★★★**, 700 years of European paintings, and ancient Middle Eastern art.

Fourth Floor – 19C and 20C decorative arts, including a Wedgewood gallery.

Fifth Floor – "American Identities: A New Look" presents works by Copley, Sargent, Cassatt, O'Keeffe and Frank Lloyd Wright alongside Native American and Spanish colonial art. You'll also find the **Elizabeth A. Sackler Center for Feminist Art★**, highlighting 40 years of women's contributions to the art world.

Prospect Park★

Main entrance at Grand Army Plaza (intersection of Flatbush Ave. & Prospect Park West). Events hot line: 718-965-8999. www.prospectpark.org.

After a visit to the museum, check out Brooklyn's most cherished park, a 526-acre wonderland of meadows and gardens designed in 1896 by Olmsted and Vaux, creators of Central Park. A road traces its periphery, and paths cut through its interior, which has plenty of ball parks and recreation facilities, as well as a carousel, a band shell, a pond and a small zoo. For lunch, exit the west side of the park and go two blocks to **Seventh Avenue**, a family-friendly strip of restaurants, cafes and boutiques.

New York Aquarium★★

W. 8th St. & Surf Ave., Coney Island. 718-265-3474. www.nyaquarium.com. Open Jun–Aug Mon–Fri 10am–6pm (weekends 7pm); rest of the year closing times vary from 4:30pm to 5:30pm. $12 ($8 ages 3–12). F or Q train to W. 8th St./New York Aquarium.

The weather outside might be frightful, but for the aquatic creatures at this indoor-outdoor facility, the water is always delightful. The first New York Aquarium—reputedly the first aquarium in the US—opened in 1896 in what is now Castle Clinton National Monument *(see Historic Sites)*. The present facility, administered by the Wildlife Conservation Society, has been a Coney Island institution since 1957. In large outdoor pools, whales, seals, sea lions, dolphins and Pacific walrus go through their paces *(check at entrance for feeding schedule)*. Indoor aquariums display more than 8,000 specimens and 300 species from around the world.

Alien Stingers★★ – This exhibit showcases sea jellies, corals and anemones.

Conservation Hall – Cownose rays glide through a floor-to-ceiling tank.

Sea Cliffs★ – The 300-foot-long North Pacific coastline habitat contains penguins, mullets, sea horses, walruses, and octopuses and other creatures, which can be viewed above and below the water.

Brooklyn Academy of Music★ *See Performing Arts.*

New York Transit Museum★

Boerum Pl. & Schermerhorn Sts., Brooklyn Heights. 718-694-1600. www.mta.info/mta/museum. Open year-round Tue–Fri 10am–4pm; Sat–Sun noon-5pm. $5. 2, 3, 4 or 5 train to Borough Hall.

Public transportation buffs will find everything they wanted to know about how New Yorkers get around in this former subway station, which houses historic subway cars, exhibits on how the tunnels were excavated, old turnstiles and more.

Coney Island – *See Musts for Kids.*

Brooklyn Tourism & Vistors Center

New to Brooklyn? Get your bearings at Brooklyn Borough Hall *(209 Joralemon St. at Court St.; open Mon–Fri 10am–6pm; 718-802-3846; www.visitbrooklyn.org)*, where you'll find neighborhood maps, hotel and restaurant listings (there are new ones cropping up every day), calendars of events, transportation information and more.

QUEENS

With an area of 120 square miles and a population topping two million, New York's biggest borough draws thousands of immigrants each year to its relatively affordable housing and its tight-knit ethnic communities—but for years it wasn't much of a draw for tourists. That is slowly changing as film studios and art museums make use of abandoned factories in the Long Island City and Astoria neighborhoods. Inland, sports thrive at **Shea Stadium** (home of the New York Mets baseball club), the **USTA National Tennis Center** (where the US Open is played each September) and **Aqueduct Racetrack** (which hosts thoroughbred horse racing). Of course, many visitors come here whether they want to or not: LaGuardia and Kennedy airports are both in Queens.

The Noguchi Museum★★

9-01 33rd Rd., at Vernon Blvd., Long Island City. 718-204-7088. www.noguchi.org. N or W train to Broadway.

The world-renowned sculptor Isamu Noguchi (1904–88) had lived and worked in a converted factory space next to this building from 1961 until 1981, when he built the present facility as a studio and museum. Noguchi, who was born in Los Angeles but raised in Japan, sculpted a range of dynamic works in New York, from the stainless-steel *News* (1938–40) for the entrance of the Associated Press building

at 50 Rockefeller Center to *The Red Cube* (1967) in the plaza in front of the Marine Midland Bank *(140 Broadway at Liberty St.)* in the Financial District. Reopened in 2004 after a two-and-a-half-year renovation, this indoor-outdoor museum displays 250 of Noguchi's sculptures in stone, wood, clay and metal, as well as working models for many of his large-scale public projects. Try to visit on a pleasant day, so you can linger in the tranquil garden.

Touring Tip

On weekends you can take a shuttle bus *($5 each way; $10 round-trip)* from the Asia Society on the Upper East Side of Manhattan directly to the Noguchi Museum and back. Queens-bound buses leave from the corner of Park Ave. and E. 70th St. at 12:30pm, 1:30pm, 2:30pm and 3:30pm. Manhattan-bound buses leave the Noguchi Museum at 2pm, 3pm, 4pm and 5pm. The trip takes approximately 30 minutes each way.

Museum for African Art★

36-01 43rd Ave. at 36th St., Long Island City. 718-784-7700. www.africanart.org. Currently closed (see below); call or check website for location and hours of traveling shows.

The only independent museum in the country dedicated to African art and culture has mounted dozens of major shows exploring Africa's artistic traditions and cultural heritage. Work has begun on the museum's new home on Fifth Avenue in Manhattan *(projected completion late 2009)*. In the meantime, the museum is curating exhibitions in a variety of locations throughout the city; check the website for schedule and construction updates.

Museum of the Moving Image★

35th Ave. at 36th St., Astoria. 718-784-0077. www.movingimage.us. Open year-round Wed–Fri 11am–5pm (Fri until 8pm), weekends 11am–6:30pm. Closed Mon & Tue; Jul 4, Thanksgiving Day & Dec 25. $10. R or V train to Steinway St. (note that V train does not run on weekends).

This eye-popping place uses its trove of film-related paraphernalia to describe the art, craft and business of making moving images. What is a moving image? Well, in AMMI's view, it's anything from a flip book to Pac-Man, though much of the space between is taken up by film. The museum was founded in 1988 in a portion of the former Kaufman Astoria Studios, which were built by Paramount Pictures in the 1920s and used by Paul Robeson, the Marx brothers and Rudolph Valentino. The studios, abandoned in 1971 and revived in the 1990s, now bustle with film and television shoots. The museum is currently undergoing a major expansion and renovation *(projected completion 2009)*; during construction, it will sponsor screenings, panel discussions and premiers at other theaters around the city *(check website for schedules and information)*.

P.S. 1 Contemporary Art Center★

22-25 Jackson Ave. at 46th Ave. 718-784-2084. www.ps1.org. Open year-round Thu–Mon noon–6pm. Closed major holidays. $5 suggested donation (free with MoMA ticket within 30 days of purchase). 7 train to Court House Square.

An affiliate of MoMA since 1999, P.S. 1 has been one of the city's most exciting venues for up-and-coming contemporary art since 1976, when it took over this 1893 school building (the "P.S." stands for "public school"). The five-story center nurtures new talent with a range of educational programs and a broad vision of what constitutes art nowadays. You'll usually find at least one site-specific installation here as well as something from MoMA, which uses the mammoth space to display large-scale works. The rest is up in the air—that's the fun of it.

STATEN ISLAND

Sometimes referred to as "the forgotten borough," Staten Island is primarily a bedroom community, sharing more in common with New Jersey than with New York. Still, the Staten Island Ferry is a thrilling—and free—ride, and while you're over there, you might as well take a look around.

Staten Island Ferry★

212-639-9675. www.siferry.com. Departs year-round daily from Whitehall Terminal at the southern tip of Manhattan about every 30min (hourly midnight–6am). 1 train to South Ferry; R or W train to Whitehall St.

Who said there were no free rides in life? The Staten Island Ferry, which shuttles commuters back and forth between Manhattan and "the forgotten borough," is free—and it offers some of the best views of Manhattan and the Statue of Liberty that you're likely to find at any price. On the five-mile voyage, which takes 25 minutes each way, the boat skirts the Statue of Liberty. On the return trip, you can zoom in on the lower New York skyline.

Alice Austen House Museum★

2 Hylan Blvd. 718-816-4506. www.aliceausten.org. Open Mar–Dec Thu–Sun noon–5pm. Closed Jan, Feb & major holidays. $2. From the ferry terminal, take S51 bus to Hylan Blvd.

Pioneer photographer Alice Austen (1866–1952) captured turn-of-the-century life in New York City, snapping elite society gatherings and immigrant scenes alike. Restored according to her own photographs, this Victorian cottage displays changing exhibits, including prints from her glass-plate negatives.

Historic Richmond Town★

441 Clarke Ave. 718-351-1611. www.historicrichmondtown.org. Open Jul–Aug Wed–Sat 10am–5pm, Sun 1pm–5pm. Rest of the year Wed–Sun 1pm–5pm. Closed Mon, Tue & major holidays. $5. From the ferry terminal, take S74 bus to Richmond Rd./St. Patrick's Pl.

Summertime is "living-history season" at this 25-acre village, with costumed interpreters demonstrating crafts (tinsmithing, printmaking) and telling stories about life in the former county seat. Don't miss the late-17C Voorlezer House, reputedly the oldest elementary school in the US.

Jacques Marchais Museum of Tibetan Art★

338 Lighthouse Ave. 718-987-3500. www.tibetanmuseum.org. Open year-round Wed–Sun 1pm–5pm. Closed major holidays. $5. From the ferry, take S74 bus to Lighthouse Ave.

This museum has a rare collection of art and artifacts from Tibet, Nepal, China, Mongolia and India. Topping Lighthouse Hill amid terraced gardens and lily ponds, the museum buildings resemble a small Buddhist mountain temple.

You'll be surprised how quickly the city melts away as you head north along the Hudson River or east out to Long Island. Drive north along US-9 and you'll discover a rich landscape of highlands and history. If you're craving the feel of sand between your toes, jump on the Long Island Parkway to reach some of the finest beaches and best-protected harbors on the Atlantic Coast.

HUDSON RIVER VALLEY★★★

Take I-87 North to I-287 West to US-9 North. Historic sites begin at Tarrytown, 30mi north of New York City. Tourist information: Hudson Valley Tourism (845-291-2136; www.travelhudsonvalley.org). Historic homes may be visited by guided tour only; check with individual sites for schedules.

A remarkable concentration of historic homes in the Hudson River Valley reflects the early-17C Dutch settlement pattern, which carved feudal estates, called "patroonships," out of the land flanking the river. When the English took over in 1664, they turned these estates into lordly manors. In the 1800s the region's wild beauty inspired artists of the Hudson River school—including Frederic Edwin Church, Thomas Cole and Albert Bierstadt—to paint massive landscapes. Today you'll find rocky crags and wooded peaks surrounding historic mansions, and small towns (Cold Spring, Rhinebeck) nestling near the riverbanks, chock-a-block with antiques stores, boutiques and bistros.

Boscobel Restoration★★

Rte. 9D, 4mi north of junction with Rte. 403, Garrison. 845-265-3638. www.boscobel.org. Open Apr–Oct Wed–Mon 9:30am–5pm. Nov–Dec Wed–Mon 9:30am–4pm. Closed Jan–Mar, Tue, Thanksgiving Day & Dec 25. $12.

Fans of the Federal style love this elegant manor, built in the early 1800s but moved in pieces to this site overlooking the Hudson in the 1950s. The restored interior features graceful arches, fireplaces embellished with classical motifs, carved woodwork and Duncan Phyfe furnishings.

The Castle on the Hudson

400 Benedict Ave., Tarrytown. 914-631-1980 or 800-616-4487. www.castleonthehudson.com. 31 rooms. Over $300. Resembling a medieval castle with its towers and arched windows, this 1910 mansion-turned-inn tops a hill overlooking the Hudson, 25 miles north of New York City. Inside, period tapestries soften the stone walls, and hand-carved four-poster beds and custom-made chandeliers decorate the guest rooms. Save time for a meal at **Equus**, where you'll dine on memorable French cuisine.

Home of FDR National Historic Site★★

Rte. 9, Hyde Park. 845-229-9115. www.nps.gov/hofr. Open year-round daily 9am–5pm. Closed Jan 1, Thanksgiving Day & Dec 25. $14 (free children under 15).

You'll feel as if you know the Roosevelt family personally after a visit to this 300-acre estate, which is bursting with historic memorabilia. Franklin Delano Roosevelt's father bought the site in 1867, and FDR was born here in 1882. In the rose garden, a simple monument of white Vermont marble marks the final resting place of FDR and his wife, Eleanor.

Kykuit★★

Rte 9 North, Sleepy Hollow. 914-631-9491. www.hudsonvalley.org. Open mid-May–early Nov Wed–Mon 9am–3pm (weekends until 4pm). Closed mid-Nov–late Apr. Tours $15–$38 depending on length.

Culinary Institute of America

1946 Campus Dr., Hyde Park. 845-471-6608. www.ciachef.edu. Here, 2,400 chefs-in-training hone their skills in five restaurants (you may be sampling the work of the next star in the culinary firmament). Reservations required.

Dutch for "lookout," Kykuit (pronounced "KYE-cut") is the most picturesque of the Hudson Valley estates; it's also one of the newest. The house was built between 1906 and 1913 by John D. Rockefeller Jr. for his father, the patriarch of Standard Oil. In all, Kykuit has housed four generations of Rockefellers. Inside you'll find antique Chinese porcelains and tapestries and a fine collection of modern art amassed by former governor Nelson Rockefeller. The lovely terraced **gardens★** contain sculptures by such artists as Picasso, Louise Nevelson and Isamu Noguchi.

West Point★★

On the west bank of the Hudson off US-9 West; take the exit for West Point/Highland Falls. 845-938-2638. www.usma.edu. Visitor center open daily 9am–4:45pm. Grounds may be visited by 1hr or 2hr guided tour only; call 845-446-4724 or go to www.westpointtours.com for schedule. $10.

The prestigious U.S. Military Academy was established here in 1802, on the site of Fortress West Point, a 1778 series of fortifications overlooking the Hudson at one of its most narrow points. In 1780 Benedict Arnold, the fort's commander, schemed to hand West Point over to the British (the plan was thwarted). In the academy's first year, 10 students graduated; today there are more than 4,200 cadets here. Try to plan your visit to coincide with one of the academy's spectacular **parades**, known for their precision of movement *(Sept–Nov & late Apr–May)*. Be sure to visit the **museum★★**, where you'll find out everything you ever wanted to know about the history of the military.

LONG ISLAND★★

Long Island boasts three major highways: The Long Island Expwy. (I-495, aka "the LIE"), the Northern State Pkwy. and the Southern State Pkwy. The Queens–Midtown Tunnel, accessible at E. 42nd St., leads directly onto the Long Island Expwy. Tourist information, including a free guide: Long Island Convention and Visitors Bureau; 631-951-3900; www.licvb.com.

From end to end, Long Island is a study in extremes. On the western tip you have ultra-urban Brooklyn and Queens; on the eastern tip, 118 miles away, lie the dramatic bluffs of Montauk. In between are vast tracts of suburban development. But that's not all. Long Island boasts many sandy beaches and seafaring towns. Although the North Shore is rockier and more dramatic than the South Shore (which is protected by several long barrier islands), both are equally worth exploring.

The Hamptons★★

South Shore, about 100mi east of New York City. www.thehamptons.com.

Home to the glitterati, Long Island's most renowned vacation spot forms a loose-knit chain of towns running 35 miles along the South Shore, from Westhampton Beach to Amagansett. Try tony **Southampton★** for superb estates and pricey shops, and the port of **Sag Harbor★** *(northeast of Southampton via Rtes. 27 & 79; www.sagharborchamber.com)* for charm. A 15-mile-long **public beach** runs from Moriches Inlet to Shinnecock Inlet.

The Long Island Museum★★

Rte. 25A at Main St., Stony Brook. 631-751-0066. www.longislandmuseum.org. Open year-round Wed–Sat 10am–5pm, Sun noon–5pm. Closed Mon, Tue & major holidays. $7 ($3 ages 6–17).

This kid-friendly complex incorporates museums of art, history and carriages, as well as a blacksmith shop, a schoolhouse and a barn. Plan on spending most of your time in the carriage museum, ogling the 250 horse-drawn carriages that range from Gypsy wagons to children's vehicles (pulled by goats or dogs).

Old Bethpage Village Restoration★★

1303 Round Swamp Rd. Old Bethpage. 516-572-8400. www.nassaucountyny.gov. Open Mar–Dec Wed–Fri 10am–4pm, weekends 10am–5pm. $7.

Take a stroll through this pre-Civil War village and watch the weaver make cloth, the farmwife prepare a meal, and farmers work their fields. More than 55 historic buildings have been moved here, creating a museum that's especially fun for families.

The Lobster Roll

1980 Montauk Hwy., Amagansett. 631-267-3740. Closed Nov–mid-Apr. Sand dunes may surround this highway shanty, but don't let the beachy atmosphere fool you. The famous lobster rolls draw the likes of Barbra Streisand, Kathleen Turner and Alec Baldwin.

Planting Fields★★

Planting Fields Rd., Oyster Bay. 516-922-8600. www.plantingfields.com. Grounds open year-round daily 9am–5pm. Closed Dec 25. $6/car (except Nov–Apr weekdays).

Flower power rules at financier William Robertson Coe's former estate, 409 acres of which have been preserved as an arboretum, with greenhouses, rolling lawns, formal gardens, hiking paths and more. The exquisite Tudor mansion may be visited by guided tour *(Apr–Sept noon–3:30pm; $6.50; 516-922-9210).*

Cold Spring Harbor Whaling Museum★

301 Main St., Cold Spring Harbor. 631-367-3418. www.cshwhalingmuseum.org. Open year-round Tue–Sun 11am–5pm, daily in summer. $5 ($4 ages 5–18).

More fun for kids, this museum brings back the town's 1850s heyday as a whaling port. Exhibits include a fully equipped 19C whaleboat, harpoons, navigational instruments, an orca skull and scrimshaw (whalebone carvings), the whaler's folk art.

Sagamore Hill National Historic Site★

Cove Neck Rd., Oyster Bay. 516-922-4447. www.nps.gov/sahi. Mansion open by guided tour only, late May–Labor Day daily 9am–5pm; rest of the year Wed–Sun 10am–4pm. Closed major holidays. $5.

Though this site includes a museum and a visitor center, the 1885 Queen Anne mansion, Teddy Roosevelt's former residence, is the main attraction here. Many of its 23 rooms appear as they did during Roosevelt's presidency (1901–09), with more than 90 percent of the family's original furnishings.

Vanderbilt Museum★

180 Little Neck Rd., Centerport. 631-854-5555. www.vanderbiltmuseum.org. Open year-round Tue–Sun noon–5pm. Closed Jan 1, Thanksgiving Day & Dec 25. $7.

William K. Vanderbilt II—"Willie K"—was a lifelong traveler, expert yachtsman and racecar driver. The 24-room, Spanish Revival-style mansion is a good setting for the natural history collections on view in the Habitat Wing. There's also a marine museum with ship models, and a planetarium.

Beaches of Long Island

Had enough of history? Then hit the beach! On the North Shore, **Sunken Meadow State Park★** *(631-269-4333; www.nysparks.com)* has a large, fine-sand beach as well as recreational activities like hiking and golf. On the South Shore you can spread your towel at **Jones Beach State Park★★** *(516-785-1600; www.nysparks.com)*, a barrier island boasting 6.5 miles of beaches along ocean and bay; car-free **Fire Island★**, which encompasses the 1,400-acre **Fire Island National Seashore★** *(631-289-4810; www.nps.gov/fiis)* and an idyllic beachfront state park; or the **Hamptons★★** *(opposite).*

The venues listed below were selected for their ambience, location and/or value for money. Rates indicate the average cost of a dinner appetizer, an entrée and a dessert for one person (not including tax, gratuity or beverages). Most restaurants accept major credit cards. Call for information regarding reservations, dress code and opening hours. For a list of restaurants by theme, see p 115. A complete listing of restaurants mentioned in this guide appears in the Index.

| Luxury | $$$$ | over $75 | Moderate | $$ | $25–$50 |
| Expensive | $$$ | $50–$75 | Inexpensive | $ | under $25 |

Luxury

Le Bernardin $$$$ Seafood

155 W. 51st St., between Sixth & Seventh Aves., Midtown. Closed Sun.
212-554-1515. www.le-bernardin.com.

Expect to spend serious money at this spacious, elegant restaurant, widely acclaimed as one of the city's best – it will be worth the splurge (the chef's tasting menu is $155, without wine). With its coffered ceiling and white-glove service, Le Bernardin also offers a prix-fixe menu that comes almost entirely from the sea. Chef Eric Ripert's delicately orchestrated dishes are divided into sections of "almost raw," "barely touched," and "lightly cooked" on the à la carte menu. Jackets required.

Chanterelle $$$$ French

2 Harrison St. at Hudson St. TriBeCa. 212-966-6960. www.chanterellenyc.com

Set inside the 19C Merchant Exchange Building, this New York classic (it's been here since 1979) serves contemporary French cuisine in a gorgeous Art Nouveau-style dining room, replete with fresh flowers. While the menu changes monthly, the signature grilled seafood sausage remains a staple. Before you leave, admire Chanterelle's collection of menu covers hanging in the little anteroom to the left of the reception desk. Over the years, distinguished artists such as Robert Mapplethorpe, Roy Lichtenstein and Louise Nevelson have designed covers for the restaurant.

Expensive

Babbo $$$ Italian

110 Waverly Pl., between Sixth Ave. & MacDougal St., Greenwich Village. Dinner only.
212-777-0303. www.babbonyc.com.

With his empire of New York City restaurants, three TV shows, and five cook-
books, Mario Batali is a household name in the restaurant world. Despite all the
demands on his time, this ponytailed chef still finds time to cook at his flagship
Greenwich Village restaurant. Although Babbo's menu changes nightly, grilled
octopus, steamed cockles with red chiles and basil, and black pepper papp-
ardelle with wild boar ragu, typify the seasonal offerings. Be sure to reserve
weeks in advance.

BLT Steak $$$ Steakhouse

106 E. 57th St., between Park & Lexington Aves., Midtown. Closed Sun. 212-752-7470.
www.bltsteak.com.

This is French chef Laurent Tourondel's version of an American steakhouse, and
a good one it is (BLT stands for Bistro Laurent Tourondel). The dining room is a
smart, contemporary space, done in black and caramel brown. On the menu,
you can pick your favorite cut of meat (Porterhouse, veal chop, rack of lamb,
New York strip) and pair it with your choice of sauces (Bernaise, blue cheese,
red wine and more). For fish lovers, there are tuna and swordfish steaks, along
with the requisite Maine lobster.

Bouley $$$ Steakhouse

120 West Broadway at Duane St., TriBeCa. 212-964-2525. www.davidbouley.com.

One of New York's finest restaurants, Bouley has two different vaulted-ceil-
inged rooms: the intimate red room, with its claret-colored Venetian-stucco
walls; or the airy white room, with its antique fireplace. The menu reflects
chef David Bouley's travels to Japan, along with his strong grounding in French
cooking techniques. If you want to take a souvenir of Bouley's food home with
you, stop in at the Bouley Market and Bakery across the street.

Café Boulud $$$ French

*20 E. 76th St., between Fifth & Madison Aves., Upper East Side. 212-772-2600.
www.danielnyc.com.*

Famed French chef Daniel Boulud pays homage to the cafe that his family owned just outside Lyon. You'll have a choice of four different tasting menus here. If you're feeling old-fashioned, choose La Tradition, made up of French country classics. If you want seasonal fare, try La Saison. For vegetarians, there's Le Potager, with market-fresh produce. Le Voyage is a menu inspired by world cuisines. Whatever he makes, Boulud exhibits creativity and intelligence in marrying diverse ingredients. The dining room is done in earth tones, with custom-designed mahogany chairs and a hammered-nickel bar.

Firebird $$$ Russian

*365 W. 46th St., between Eighth & Ninth Aves., Midtown. Closed Mon. 212-586-0244.
www.firebirdrestaurant.com.*

Tsar Nicholas would no doubt feel as comfortable in these three elegantly restored town houses as he did in the Winter Palace, and would probably enjoy the cuisine as much, too—with dishes like Ukrainian borscht, poached sturgeon and chicken Kiev, plus seven kinds of caviar. It's a fun place to eat with the pre-theater crowd before walking over to a Broadway show. Stick around for the complementary jazz at the adjacent Firebird Lounge.

Gotham Bar and Grill $$$ American

*12 E. 12th St., between Fifth Ave. & University Pl., Union Square. 212-260-4020.
www.gothambarandgrill.com.*

Gotham is consistently rated one of New York's finest restaurants, and for good reason. Executive chef Alfred Portale fits New York to a T. The pioneer of vertical cuisine, he creates innovative, towering "skyscraper" presentations that are a treat for the eye as well as the palate. Seafood salad is a high-rise concoction of lobster, scallops, octopus, squid and avocado, crowned with a ruffle of purple lettuce. Even the rich chocolate desserts stand at attention. One of the best culinary bargains in town is Gotham's $25 prix-fixe lunch.

Keens Steakhouse $$$ Steakhouse

*72 W. 36th St., between Fifth & Sixth Aves.,
Garment District. Dinner only Sat & Sun.
212-947-3636. www.keens.com.*

A carnivore's delight, Keens serves up big slabs of prime rib, steaks and lamb in a historic setting. The restaurant opened in 1885, when Herald Square—which is around the corner—was still the city's Theater District. Keens started out as a men's dining, drinking and pipe-smoking club for the city's movers and shakers at the turn of the century; hanging from the ceiling is the world's biggest collection of churchwarden clay pipes.

Nobu Next Door
$$$ Japanese

105 Hudson St. at Franklin St., TriBeCa. Dinner only. 212-334-4445.
www.myriadrestaurantgroup.com.

Although it's nearly impossible to get a table at the highly acclaimed **Nobu**, you can sample essentially the same food at Nobu Next Door located right next to the parent restaurant. The emphasis here is on texture—its well-crafted sushi bar of black river rocks, tables of scorched pine and Indonesian market-basket light fixtures harmonize with the sensual pleasures of clawless lobsters, sea urchins, seafood udon (noodles) and mochi ice-cream balls. Nobu Next Door doesn't take reservations—go early to avoid a long wait.

Park Avenue Cafe
$$$ Contemporary

100 E. 63rd St. at Park Ave., Upper East Side. 212-644-1900.
www.parkavenuecafe.com.

This friendly neighborhood cafe welcomes diners to relax on cheery red-and-white-striped banquettes amid crimson walls. Chef Neil Murphy, who trained at the Culinary Institute of America, highlights fresh regional products such as the crispy top Chatham cod, and tastings of farm harvest vegetables. A list of more than 250 wines complements the cuisine, and the restaurant offers a generous selection of wines by the glass.

Perry Street
$$$ Contemporary

176 Perry St. at West St., West Village. 212-352-1900. www.jean-georges.com.

Marked by impeccable service, sleek surroundings and flawlessly prepared food, Perry Street may well be Jean-Georges Vongerichten's most appealing restaurant. Sink deep into one of the snug chairs or banquettes and turn your eye to the French-inflected New American menu. Seafood is a specialty, and the desserts are divine. The $24 prix-fixe lunch is one of the best deals in town.

Union Square Cafe
$$$ Italian

21 E. 16th St., between Fifth Ave. & Union Sq. W., Union Square. 212-243-4020.

Open since 1985, this popular bistro—restaurateur Danny Meyer's flagship—still packs in crowds every night. It's not hard to see why: the service is friendly and impeccable, the surroundings cool and comfortable, the food imaginative. Executive chef Michael Romano dishes up a selection of entrées—like creamy crab risotto, or cod with seasoned lentils—as well as daily specials (osso buco, for instance, is only served on Sunday). Don't have a reservation? Belly up to the bar for the same food in a more casual setting.

Moderate

Blue Ribbon Sushi $$ Japanese

119 Sullivan St. between Prince and Spring Sts., SoHo. 212-343-0404.
www.blueribbonrestaurants.com.

A downtown sushi mainstay, Blue Ribbon Sushi has a vast menu of fresh and
buttery raw fish, as well as a kids' menu of assorted yakimono and maki (there's
even fried chicken and catfish fingers). Thanks to its no-reservations policy, the
waits at the SoHo flagship can be long. If you happen to be staying in Brooklyn,
though, you can sample the same grub at the Park Slope outpost *(278 Fifth Ave.
between First St. and Garfield Pl., 718-840-0408).*

The Boathouse $$ Contemporary

*In Central Park (E. 72nd St. & Park Dr. N.), Upper East Side. Lunch year-round. Dinner
Apr–Nov only. 212-517-2233. www.thecentralparkboathouse.com.*

You couldn't dream up a more romantic setting for a first date or an
anniversary celebration. Nestled on
the shore of the lake in the middle
of Central Park, the Boathouse
offers peaceful water views to go
along with dishes like jumbo lump
crab cakes served with cornichon
and caper remoulade to pan-roasted
pork tenderloin. On sunny days, sit
out on the deck and watch the
rowboats drift by. After lunch, you
can rent one and take a spin for
yourself.

El Cid $$ Spanish

322 W. 15th St. between Eighth & Ninth Aves., Chelsea. 212-929-9332.

Family-owned and run, this unpretentious neighborhood eatery is one of the
best spots in the city to get tapas (appetizer-size portions of Spanish dishes)
and fresh sangria. The simple setting belies the restaurant's location in the hip-
for-the-moment Meatpacking District. The dozen tables are jammed together
and the bar is crowded, so be sure to make reservations to sample tasty tapas
like white aparagus in vinaigrette, baby eels, grilled shrimp and more.

The Fatty Crab $$ Malaysian

643 Hudson St. between Gansevoort & Horatio Sts., Meatpacking District. 212-352-3590.
www.fattycrab.com.

Though it's only a few years old, this diminutive restaurant feels like it's been
around forever with its dark, well-worn interior, rock music and fanatical following,
which keeps the place noisy and crowded at all hours. But chef Zak Pellacio takes
the food seriously, having spent time in Malaysia perfecting his craft. The chili crab
is excellent, with large pieces of Dungeness crab in a spicy-sweet tomato chili
sauce; so is the fatty duck.

Good Enough to Eat $$ American

483 Amsterdam Ave. between W. 83rd & W. 84th Sts., Upper West Side. 212-496-0163. www.goodenoughtoeat.com.

A white picket fence marks the entrance to this homey little place with its exposed-brick walls and folk art accents. Comfort food –just like Mom used to make–stars on the menu, which features perennial favorites such as meatloaf, pumpkin pie and turkey dinner with all the trimmings. Portions are huge, so go with an appetite.

Il Palazzo $$ Italian

151 Mulberry St. between Grand & Hester Sts., Little Italy. 212-343-7000.

Right on Little Italy's main drag, Il Palazzo dishes up a generous selection of classics: veal saltimbocca, chicken cacciatore, rigatoni alla vodka, linguine with clam sauce, shrimp scampi. End your meal with a glass of grappa or vintage port and then head around the corner to Ferrara *(195 Grand St.)* bakery for espresso and gelato.

Les Halles Downtown $$ French

15 John St. between Broadway & Nassau Sts., Financial District. 212-285-8585. www.leshalles.net.

Chef/author Anthony Bourdain (who penned the restaurant exposé *Kitchen Confidential*) opened this restaurant after the terrorist attack of September 11, 2001 – one of the first new restaurants to open in the Financial District at the time. Here he serves up such palate-pleasing French dishes as steak au poivre and coq au vin. You'll find basically the same menu at his other brasserie, Les Halls on Park Avenue *(411 Park Ave., between E 28th & 29th Sts.; 212-679-4111).*

Macelleria $$ Italian

48 Gansevoort St. between Greenwich & Washington Sts., Meatpacking District. 212-741-2555. www.macelleriarestaurant.com.

Housed in a reconstructed butcher shop, this engaging trattoria with its brick-walled wine cellar offers an outstanding variety of salami, homemade pastas, meat dishes and Italian wines. Start with the iceberg lettuce wedge with gorgonzola and peppercorn dressing, then move on to a pasta dish such as green and white tagliolini with peas and prosciutto, or garganelli with oxtail ragu.

Marseille $$ Mediterranean

630 Ninth Ave. at W. 44th St., Theater District. 212-333-3410. www.marseillenyc.com.

Located within walking distance of Times Square, Marseille is a terrific spot for pre- and post-theater dining. Serving French cuisine with Moroccan, Turkish and Tunisian overtones, Marseille's Art Deco setting with its pastel arches, handmade floor tiles and old zinc bar makes you think you're on the set of *Casablanca*. Marseille's menu runs the gamut from bouillabaisse to lamb tagine. Broadway headliners often drop by after performances.

Odeon
$$ American

145 West Broadway between Thomas & Duane Sts., TriBeCa. 212-233-0507.
www.theodeonrestaurant.com.

A TriBeCa hot spot since the early 1980s, Odeon has long been a place where the glitterati come to eat. You may still catch a glimpse of big-name entertainers and artists here, but the real draw is the refined cuisine, especially the weekday fixed-price menu at lunch. If you're interested in dining at odd hours, Odeon serves a brasserie menu of light fare daily from 4pm to 5:30pm, and from midnight until 2am every night.

Sarabeth's Restaurant
$$ American

423 Amsterdam Ave. at W. 80th St., Upper West Side. 212-496-6280; Check website for other locations in Midtown and on the Upper East Side. www.sarabeth.com.

Although Sarabeth's serves breakfast, lunch and dinner, it's most popular in the morning hours and for brunch on weekends. Breakfast fare includes porridge, fluffy omelets, muffins, pancakes and waffles. Try the Four Flowers juice—a blend of banana, pineapple, orange and pomegranate. Sarabeth's also sells a selection of its award-winning baked goods and preserves, which make great souvenirs.

Spotted Pig
$$ Gastropub

314 W. 11th St. at Greenwich St., West Village. 212-620-0390. www.thespottedpig.com.

One of the city's most popular restaurants, the Spotted Pig sports a country-cute decor that still manages to be hip, with rustic tables covered in butcher-block paper, pig paraphernalia and other bric-a-brac. Celebrities abound—Bill Clinton allegedly waited a half-hour for a table—but the food's the real star here, with young British-expat chef April Bloomfield turning out robust fare like fried calf livers and rabbit stew. Come early (before 6pm) to avoid the horrendous line; reservations are not accepted. Also be aware that vegetarian options are limited.

Tamarind
$$ Indian

41–43 E. 22nd St. between Broadway & Park Ave., Union Square. 212-674-7400.
www.tamarinde22.com.

There's no mistaking the setting at Tamarind — there are reminders of India everywhere. Cowbells hang in the alcoves of the gleaming-white dining room; a large, wrought-iron wall hanging from a maharaja's palace greets guests at the entrance. Bustling cooks prepare piquant regional Indian dishes in the glassed-in kitchen. And a good, balanced wine list and a staff of smiling, attentive servers add to Tamarind's appeal. For lighter, less expensive fare, go to the tea house next door.

Inexpensive

Angelica Kitchen $ Vegan

300 E. 12th St., between First & Second Aves., East Village. 212-228-2909.
www.angelicakitchen.com.

Health-conscious New Yorkers love the creative vegan
fare (no meat or dairy) at this popular East Village eatery.
Most of the dishes are simply prepared, letting the flavors
of the vegetables (usually local and organic) speak for
themselves. Many diners cobble together dinner from the
wide assortment of salads, grilled vegetables, tofu and
breads (the rice-dense cornbread is a meal in itself), though the most flavorful
dishes are often the daily specials, which range from savory stews to tamales.

Azuri Café $ Falafel

465 W. 51st St. between Ninth & Tenth Aves., Midtown. 212-262-2920.

Don't expect to be wined and dined at this Hell's Kitchen hole-in-the-wall; the
atmosphere is pretty much nonexistent. But for fresh, savory middle Eastern
food, including some of the best falafel, tabouli and baba ghanoush you'll find
in New York, Azuri can't be beat. Grab a root beer from the cooler and order
one of the plates, which will give you an entrée (try the falafel or the vegeta-
ble patties) with an assortment of salads and fresh pita bread.

Carnegie Delicatessen $ Jewish Kosher

854 Seventh Ave. between W. 54th & W. 55th Sts., Midtown. 212-757-2245.
www.carnegiedeli.com.

It's hard to tell what this kosher deli is more famous for: salty service or mile-
high pastrami sandwiches. It's best to endure the former for the latter — split a
sandwich if you want, to save room for the delicious cheesecake. Be prepared
to share your table here, it's all part of the fun.

Dim Sum Go Go $ Chinese

5 E. Broadway at Chatham Square, Chinatown. 212-732-0797.

Don't let the Chinese take-out name throw you. This sleek restaurant is more
sophisticated than many of its Uptown counterparts. New-wave dim sum is
served to order, not on traditional rolling carts. Mushroom and pickled-veg-
etable dumplings, duck skin and crabmeat wrapped in spinach dough, or chive
and shrimp dumplings in a ginger-vinegar dipping sauce are just a few of the
many choices.

Full Shilling $ Irish Pub

160 Pearl St. (Wall–Pine Sts.), Financial District. 212-422-3855. www.thefullshilling.com.

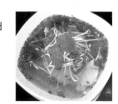

The Full Shilling serves up traditional Irish pub food,
including bangers and mash, shepherd's pie and fish and
chips, in a traditional Irish pub setting just steps from
the power corridor of Wall Street. Something about
the dim lighting, the clatter of plates and the friendly
service seems to melt away stress. A couple of (impe-
rial) pints don't hurt either.

Great N.Y. Noodletown
$ Chinese

28 Bowery at Bayard St., Chinatown. 212-349-0923.

If it's tasty, inexpensive Chinese food you seek, you can't go wrong here. This is a casual place: the menu is displayed under the pane of glass that tops the table and you pay the cashier before you leave. Noodles dominate the menu. You can get them pan-fried, Cantonese-style, or in Hong Kong-style lo mein. There's also a wide choice of salt-baked dishes and barbecued meats.

'inoteca
$ Italian

98 Rivington St. at Ludlow St., Lower East Side. 212-614-0473. www.inotecanyc.com.

Magnet for the chic young Lower East Side set, this clamorous restaurant offers a superb selection of well-priced Italian wines—some 250 in all—from every region of Italy (an enoteca is a "wine bar" in Italy). Of these, 25 are available by the glass. The menu stars small plates and panini (stuffed with the likes of fontina and arugula, or roasted vegetables and fresh ricotta). For a more soothing atmosphere (albeit a tighter squeeze), try sister restaurant **'ino** in Greenwich Village *(21 Bedford St., between Downing St. & Sixth Ave.; 212-989-5796)*.

John's Pizzeria
$ Italian

260 W. 44th St. (between Broadway & Eighth Ave.), Midtown. 212-391-7560. See website for other locations. www.johnspizzerianyc.com.

New York has hundreds of pizzerias, but John's takes the quality of the product up a notch by baking its thin-crust pies in brick ovens, going easy on the cheese and offering a wide selection of fresh vegetables and other toppings. John's serves whole pies only—no slices—so come with an appetite. There's also an enticing array of stuffed rolls, salads and Italian sandwiches. The cavernous Times Square location is as vast as the Greenwich village shop is teeny.

Pó
$ Italian

31 Cornelia St., between Bleecker & W. 4th Sts, Greenwich Village. 212-654-2189. www.porestaurant.com.

Specializing in Tuscan fare with a well-selected, moderately priced wine list, this snug Italian trattoria makes diners feel like guests at a delightful dinner party. The value for money here is hard to beat. For dinner, try pasta (white bean ravioli with brown butter sauce, or linguine with fresh clams and white wine). Chef Lee McGrath's six-course tasting menu is a great deal at only $48.

Soba-Ya
$ Japanese

229 E. Ninth St. between First & Second Aves, East Village. 212-533-6966.

Soba-Ya's inexpensive noodle dishes and Zen-like atmosphere appeal to students from nearby New York University. On a cold day, nothing warms you up like a steaming bowl of housemade buckwheat noodles swimming in broth and topped with meat and vegetables. In warm weather, try your noodles cold with add-ons heaped on top.

Another Way to Look at It: Restaurants by Theme

Whether you're looking for just the right spot for a special occasion, a restaurant with a celebrity chef, the perfect place for brunch or a neighborhood gem, New York's got it. In the previous pages we've organized the restaurants by price category; here we've arranged them by theme to help you find the perfect place to eat. All restaurants listed below are in Manhattan.

Bring the Kids
Carnegie Delicatessen *(p 113)*
Dim Sum Go Go *(p 113)*
El Cid *(p 110)*
John's Pizzeria *(p 114)*
Great N.Y.
 Noodletown *(p 114)*

Brunch Spots
Carnegie Delicatessen *(p 113)*
Good Enough to Eat *(p 111)*
Sarabeth's Restaurant *(p 112)*
Park Avenue Cafe *(p 109)*

Celebrity Chefs
Babbo (Mario Batali) *(p 107)*
Bouley
 (David Bouley) *(p 107)*
Café Boulud
 (Daniel Boulud) *(p 108)*
Gotham Bar and Grill
 (Alfred Portale) *(p 108)*
Le Bernardin
 (Eric Ripert) *(p 106)*
Les Halles Downtown
 (Anthony Bourdain)
 (p 111)
Nobu Next Door
 (Nobu Matsuhisa) *(p 109)*
Perry Street (Jean-Georges
Vongerichten) *(p 109)*

Easy on the Budget
Angelica Kitchen *(p 113)*
Azuri Cafe *(p 113)*
Carnegie Delicatessen *(p 113)*
Dim Sum Go Go *(p 113)*
Great N.Y.
 Noodletown *(p 114)*
'inoteca *(p 114)*
John's Pizzeria *(p 114)*
Pó *(p 114)*
Soba-Ya *(p 114)*

Hip Scenes
'inoteca *(p 114)*
Nobu Next Door *(p 109)*
Odeon *(p 112)*
Gotham Bar and Grill *(p 108)*
Spotted Pig *(p 112)*
Union Square Café *(p 109)*

Neighborhood Favorites
Carnegie Delicatessen *(p 113)*
El Cid *(p 110)*
Great N.Y. Noodletown
 (p 114)
Il Palazzo *(p 111)*
'inoteca *(p 114)*
Pó *(p 114)*
Union Square Cafe *(p 109)*

Outdoor Seating (seasonal)
Boathouse at
 Central Park *(p 110)*
Good Enough to Eat *(p 111)*

Pre-Theater Dining
Firebird *(p 108)*
Marseille *(p 111)*

Quick Bites
Azuri Cafe *(p 113)*
John's Pizzeria *(p 114)*
Soba-Ya *(p 114)*

Special-Occasion Restaurants
Boathouse at
 Central Park *(p 110)*
Bouley *(p 107)*
Chanterelle *(p 106)*
Gotham Bar and Grill *(p 108)*
Le Bernardin *(p 106)*

Steakhouses
BLT Steak *(p 107)*
Keens Steakhouse *(p 108)*

The properties listed below were selected for their ambience, location and/or value for money. Prices reflect the average cost for a standard double room for two people in high season. Hotels in New York often offer special discount rates on weekends and off-season. Quoted rates don't include New York City's hotel tax of 13.62% and the $3.50 per room per night surcharge. For a list of hotels by theme, see p 124. A complete listing of hotels mentioned in this guide appears in the Index.

Luxury	$$$$$	over $350	Moderate	$$$	$175–$250
Expensive	$$$$	$250–$350	Inexpensive	$$	$100–$175

Luxury

Inn at Irving Place $$$$$ 12 rooms

56 Irving Pl., between E. 17th & E. 18th Sts., Gramercy Park. 212-533-4600 or 800-685-1447. www.innatirving.com.

You won't find the name of the inn on these two 1834 brownstones; just look for the address. Within you will find stylish guest rooms appointed with high-quality 19C furnishings (four-poster beds, overstuffed chairs) as well as up-to-the-minute technology, including wireless Internet access. Continental breakfast is served in the cozy parlor. Afternoon tea, a real treat, is served in Lady Mendl's Victorian tea salon *(reservations required)*. Martinis and nibbles can be had in the downstairs lounge.

Ritz-Carlton New York, Central Park $$$$$ 261 rooms

50 Central Park South at Sixth Ave., Midtown. 212-308-9100. www.ritzcarlton.com.

With unrivaled views of Central Park and the city skyline, this Ritz-Carlton provides the ultimate in luxury and service. Stand-out amenities include complimentary limo service in Midtown; telescopes and birding books in park-view rooms; DVD players and a library of Academy Award–winning films; and complimentary use of Burberry trench coats for guests—even canine ones—when needed. La Prairie Switzerland has opened its first American full-service luxury day spa here, and **Atelier ($$$)** with its New French cuisine rates as one of the finest restaurants in New York *(jackets required)*.

The Royalton $$$$$ 169 rooms

44 W. 44th St., between Fifth & Sixth Aves., Midtown. 212-869-4400 or 800-635-9013.
www.ianschragerhotels.com.

In contrast to its historic 1898 exterior, the inside of the Royalton is daringly modern. Opened in 1988, it's the first New York product of avant-garde hotelier Ian Schrager and designer Philippe Starck. Sleek, well-appointed guest rooms all have CD players and refrigerator/minibars. Wireless Internet access is available for a fee. Bathrooms have slate- and glass-walled showers or five-foot-wide circular tubs. The lobby bars draw a stylish crowd after 5pm.

Waldorf-Astoria Hotel $$$$$ 1,423 rooms

301 Park Ave., between E. 49th & E. 50th Sts., Midtown. 212-355-3000 or 800-925-3673.
www.waldorfastoria.com.

Having been recently renovated to the tune of $400 million and taken over by the Hilton Hotel chain, the 1931 Art Deco Waldorf-Astoria remains one of New York City's most enduring symbols of luxury. Even today, casual dress (cutoff jeans, tank tops, T-shirts) is not permitted in the marble-floored lobby, where guests can tap into free wireless Internet service. Well-appointed rooms are individually decorated; spacious units in the exclusive Waldorf Towers are known for their exquisite European furnishings and butler service.

Expensive

Algonquin Hotel $$$$ 174 rooms

59 W. 44th St., between Fifth & Sixth Aves., Midtown. 212-840-6800 or 800-555-8000.
www.algonquinhotel.com.

This quiet hotel was the site of Alexander Woollcott's famous Algonquin Round Table, a 1920s gathering place for a celebrated clique of writers, including Dorothy Parker and Robert Benchley. A refurbishing in 1998 gave all its guest rooms new fittings. The Algonquin's popular cabaret bar, the Oak Room, hosts some of the country's top vocal jazz acts; the Roundtable Restaurant has a moderately priced pre-theater menu, and the Blue Bar offers casual dining. Literary types can borrow an iPod loaded with the latest audio books.

Hotel 57
$$$$ 118 rooms

30 E. 57th St. at Lexington Ave., Midtown. 212-753-8841 or 800-497-6028.
www.stayinnny.com.

This stylish, pet-friendly hotel is one of three New York properties owned by the Citylife Hotel Group. Rooms are decorated in earth tones and boast Egyptian linens, flat-screen TVs, writing desks and CD players; wireless Internet access is available at an additional charge. For shoppers and sightseers, the location is ideal. From here, it's an easy walk to Central Park, 57th Street galleries, Madison Avenue, Fifth Avenue and Museum Mile.

Iroquois Hotel
$$$$ 114 rooms

49 W. 44th St., between Fifth & Sixth Aves., Midtown. 212-840-3080. www.iroquoisny.com.

The Iroquois is convenient for Broadway theaters and Times Square. Bathrooms are outfitted with Italian marble, and robes and linens are by Frette. James Dean, star of *Rebel Without a Cause*, used to bunk here when he was a struggling actor (and rates were much lower!). If you order room service, request a complimentary film—either made in New York, directed by a New Yorker or starring a New Yorker—to be delivered on your tray.

The Mansfield
$$$$ 124 rooms

12 W. 44th St. at Fifth Ave., Midtown. 212-944-6050 or 800-255-5167.
www.mansfieldhotel.com.

Boutique-hotel warmth meld with old-world sophistication at this posh property. Complimentary espresso and cappuccino are available 24 hours a day. Rooms come with high-speed Internet access, down comforters and pillows, Belgian linens, plush towels and robes, Aveda products and DVD and CD players (music and films available free of charge). The sleek M Bar on the ground floor draws an upscale after-work crowd and offers live jazz on Wednesday and Thursday; order appetizers here at night and breakfast in the morning.

New York Palace
$$$$ 896 rooms

455 Madison Ave., between E. 50th & E. 51st Sts., Midtown. 212-888-7000 or
800-697-2522. www.newyorkpalace.com.

Enter this 55-story skyscraper through the 19C Villard Houses *(see Historic Sites)*, opposite Saint Patrick's Cathedral. Just inside, note the mansion's original molded ceiling before descending the grand staircase into the marble-columned lobby. Oversize guest rooms are decorated with gold-brocade bedspreads. A 7,000 sq ft fitness center gives guests good options for exercise.

Westin New York at Times Square

$$$$ 863 rooms

270 W. 43rd St. at Eighth Ave., Midtown. 212-201-2700 or 800-837-4183. www.westinny.com.

Westin New York is the most dramatically designed hotel to hit New York in a decade. Arquitectonica of Miami designed this attention-grabber: A soaring beam of light curves up the 42nd Street side of the structure at night and appears to pierce the sky. Guest rooms boast sleek furnishings and bold abstract art on muted wall coverings. The health club offers a panoramic view of the city, and "one call does it all" permits guests to dial just one number to have any request fulfilled. **Shula's Steak House ($$$$$)** specializes in serving the "biggest and best" cuts of certified Angus beef.

W New York

$$$$ 751 rooms

541 Lexington Ave., between E. 49th & E. 50th Sts., Midtown. 212-755-1200. www.whotels.com.

Earth, wind, fire and water are the cardinal elements that inspired this hotel's peaceful ambience. Soothing natural light filters through the two-story lobby, a cozy space with clusters of comfortable couches and a magazine rack. Relaxing earth tones, fluffy featherbeds and top-quality amenities compensate for the small bedrooms. The Heartbeat restaurant serves healthy fare. Drop by the stylish Whiskey Blue lounge, adjacent to the lobby, for a nightcap.

Moderate

Avalon

$$$ 100 rooms

16 E. 32nd St., between Madison & Fifth Aves., Murray Hill. 212-299-7000. www.theavalonny.com.

In the shadow of the Empire State Building, the Avalon opened in 1998 in a building that was totally rebuilt on the inside. Today it's an elegant, luxurious boutique hotel with traditional comforts and modern technology (all suites have high-speed Internet access). Most guest accommodations are suites, averaging more than 450 square feet. **Avalon Grill ($$)** serves New American cuisine, and breakfast is included in the room rate.

Bentley Hotel

$$$ 197 rooms

500 E. 62nd St. at York Ave., Upper East Side. 212-644-6000 or 888-664-6835. www.nychotels.com.

The Bentley's rooftop restaurant lounge has views of the city, but then so do many rooms in this sleek yet reasonably priced hotel. Rooms have floor-to-ceiling windows, custom-designed contemporary furniture, CD players, on-demand movies and down comforters. Discounted parking is available. Complimentary continental breakfast is served each morning in the lobby, where there's also a 24-hour espresso bar. Walk to Bloomingdale's and Museum Mile.

Excelsior Hotel $$$ 198 rooms

45 W. 81st St., between Central Park West & Columbus Ave., Upper West Side. 212-362-9200. www.excelsiorhotelny.com.

Overlooking the American Museum of Natural History, this newly renovated hotel excels at making guests feel at home. Ask the concierge for help with restaurant reservations and theater tickets. One- and two-bedroom suites, done up in country-French décor, contain plush bathrobes and in-room safes. The on-site health club offers a good selection of workout machines.

Hotel 41 at Times Square $$$ 47 rooms

206 W. 41st St., between Seventh & Eighth Aves., Midtown. 212-703-8600. www.hotel41.com.

Opened in 2002, Hotel 41 is a cozy, reasonably priced boutique hotel that's just steps from "the crossroads of the world" (Times Square). All rooms come with luxurious amenities such as a private safe, bottled water, Belgian linens, down pillows, Frette robes, CD/DVD players, daily newspaper of your choice and high-speed Internet access. Choose a movie or CD from the lending library and enjoy a drink (either a glass of Chardonnay or a Manhattan) on the house before going out and painting the town red. Well-behaved pets are welcome.

Hotel Chandler $$$ 123 rooms

12 E. 31st St., between Fifth & Madison Aves., Murray Hill. 212-889-6363 or 866-627-7847. www.hotelchandler.com.

Close to the Empire State Building, Madison Square Garden and Penn Station, Hotel Chandler offers understated elegance at a reasonable price. Black-and-white photographs of New York street scenes decorate the walls of spacious rooms, where the bed is wrapped in Frette linens and the bath is stocked with Aveda toiletries. Other amenities include overnight shoeshine service and a 24-hour fitness center and sauna. Intimate Bar 12:31 serves breakfast, light lunch and evening snacks, and is a favorite with budding models.

Hotel Chelsea $$$ 250 rooms

222 W. 23rd St., between Seventh & Eighth Aves., Chelsea. 212-243-3700. www.hotelchelsea.com.

The Chelsea's redbrick Victorian structure, with its wrought-iron balconies, dominates its block on West 23rd Street. Rooms all have private baths and cable TV, but otherwise this is a no-frills hotel with a number of permanent residents. Once home to Thomas Wolfe, Arthur Miller, Dylan Thomas and other literary luminaries, the hotel is listed on the National Register of Historic Places. The old-fashioned lobby's huge wooden fireplace contrasts with the modern art hanging on every wall.

Hotel Pennsylvania $$$ 1,700 rooms

401 Seventh Ave., between W. 32nd & 33rd Sts., Garment District. 212-736-5000 or 800-223-8585. www.hotelpenn.com.

Across the street from Madison Square Garden and Penn Station, and a short walk from Macy's, the Pennsylvania is one of New York's largest hotels. It was recently renovated, as seen in its modern, bustling marble-pillared lobby with mirrored walls. The labyrinthine corridors in its 17 floors of guest rooms can be daunting, but the large number of rooms makes the hotel quite affordable by New York standards. There's a sightseeing and airport-transportation desk in the lobby and plenty of amenities for business travelers.

Hudson Hotel
$$$ 1,000 rooms

356 W. 58th St., between Eighth & Ninth Aves., Midtown. 212-554-6000 or 800-697-1791. www.hudsonhotel.com.

The super-stylish Hudson offers a wide array of services and in-room amenities for a reasonable price. The tradeoff—guest rooms are very small even by New York City standards. A short walk from the Theater District and Lincoln Center, The Hudson is another Ian Schrager–Philippe Starck collaboration that has drawn attention for its unique and creative public spaces. Its restaurant, the Hudson Cafeteria, features communal tables;  the rooftop garden boasts hot tubs; and the glass-floored Hudson Bar overflows with hip young customers.

The Lucerne
$$$ 280 rooms

201 W. 79th St. at Amsterdam Ave., Upper West Side. 212-875-1000 or 800-492-8122. www.newyorkhotel.com.

Set in an historic 1903 building in the heart of the Upper West Side, the Lucerne has been transformed into a modern, European-style boutique hotel with spacious guest rooms and a full slate of amenities, from in-room movies to marble bathrooms and a fitness center. **Nice Matin ($$$)** features fine Mediterranean cuisine. Stroll the brownstone-lined side streets to the American Museum of Natural History and Central Park.

Inexpensive

Amsterdam Inn
$$ 28 rooms

340 Amsterdam Ave. at W. 76th St., Upper West Side. 212-579-7500. www.amsterdaminn.com.

For a simple quarters at a bargain price, try the Amsterdam Inn. A residential building converted to hotel use in 1999, the inn has some rooms with shared baths, some with private facilities. All have color TV, air conditioning, phones and maid service. Some rooms have kitchenettes. Be prepared to carry your luggage up a few flights of stairs—the hotel has four floors and no elevator; a doorman can assist you during the day. It's a short walk to the Museum of Natural History, Central Park and Lincoln Center.

Best Western Seaport Inn $$ 72 rooms

33 Peck Slip at Front St., Financial District. 212-766-6600 or 800-468-3569.
www.seaportinn.com.

This lower-priced lodging has several things going for it. It's within easy walking distance of popular attractions like South Street Seaport, the Staten Island Ferry, and Battery Park. It sits near the colorful district where the Fulton Fish Market once resided, complete with cobblestone streets. And its sixth- and seventh-floor rooms come with a terrace that offers incredible views of the East River and Brooklyn Bridge. Done up country-style with floral prints, guest quarters are well-maintained and comfortable. You'll be treated to a continental breakfast in the morning and cookies each afternoon. High-speed Internet access is available at no charge.

Cosmopolitan Hotel $$ 122 rooms

95 West Broadway at Chambers St., TriBeCa. 212-566-1900. www.cosmohotel.com.

The longest continuously operated hotel in New York City, dating back to 1850, the Cosmopolitan is located in the heart of TriBeCa, within easy walking distance of the World Trade Center Site, City Hall, SoHo and Chinatown. Rooms are newly renovated, with private baths and color television. Best of all, a wealth of shopping and dining options lie within a five-block radius.

Gershwin Hotel $$ 150 rooms

7 E. 27th St., between Madison & Fifth Ave., Flatiron District. 212-545-8000.
www.gershwinhotel.com.

Young international travelers, as well as up-and-coming models and families, are drawn to this funky little hotel in the Flatiron District. Though the building dates back 100 years, the décor recalls Andy Warhol and his Pop Art brethren. For families there are two creatively appointed suites, as well as baby-sitting services. It's a five-minute walk to the Empire State Building. For the budget-conscious, there are a few dorm-style rooms with shared baths.

Hotel Belleclaire $$ 170 rooms

250 W. 77th St. at Broadway, Upper West Side. 212-362-7700 or
877-468-3522. www.hotelbelleclaire.com.

Built in 1903, this Upper West Side landmark has been home to Mark Twain and Maxim Gorky. Tastefully designed rooms boast goose-down comforters. The staff is friendly and helpful, and the brand-new fitness center is free for guests. Walk to Central Park and Lincoln Center, or just stroll the neighborhood—the tree-lined side streets are some of New York's most inviting. For breakfast, get a homemade bagel from nearby Zabar's *(see Must Shop).*

Larchmont Hotel $$ 60 rooms

27 W. 11th St., between Fifth & Sixth Aves., Greenwich Village. 212-989-9333.
www.larchmonthotel.com.

You're smack in the middle of Greenwich Village when you stay at this trim, well-maintained property. Rooms are amply outfitted with ceiling fans and blonde furnishings, accented by maroon fabrics and carpeting. Guests are provisioned with a robe and slippers—and a complimentary continental breakfast with freshly baked goodies. The drawback? Even though rooms come with a wash basin, bathrooms are down the hall and must be shared.

Manhattan Seaport Suites Hotel
$$ 56 rooms

129 Front St. (between Wall & Pine Sts.), Financial District. 212-742-0003.
www.seaportsuites.com.

South Street Seaport, the Staten Island Ferry, Wall Street and other Financial District sites are all nearby this small, friendly hotel, which offers rooms as well as suites. Studios and one-bedrooms have kitchenettes and sitting rooms; many also feature skylights and hardwood floors. All have complimentary wireless Internet access. Continental breakfast is served each morning, and coffee, tea and hot chocolate are available for guests 24 hours a day.

Mayfair New York
$$ 78 rooms

242 W. 49th St. (between Broadway & Eighth Ave.), Midtown. 212-586-0300 or
800-556-2932. www.mayfairnewyork.com.

One of the few family-run hotels in Manhattan, the hospitable and gently priced Mayfair is located in the heart of the Theater District. Guest rooms and common areas showcase a collection of rare historic photos from the Museum of the City of New York; double-pane windows filter out street noise. Amenities include fresh-cut flowers and wall safes.

Pickwick Arms
$$ 368 rooms

230 E. 51st. St. (between Second & Third Aves.), Midtown. 212-355-0300 or 800-742-5945.
www.pickwickarms.com.

You can't find a better East Side hotel bargain than the Pickwick. What the accommodations lack in size they make up for by being on a lovely residential block convenient to Saint Patrick's Cathedral, Rockefeller Center, and Grand Central Terminal. The attractiveness of the rooms varies widely; ask for one that has been recently renovated. (If you want a real deal, get one with a shared bath.) Be sure to check out the charming rooftop garden.

Washington Square Hotel
$$ 165 rooms

103 Waverly Pl. at Washington Square West,
Greenwich Village. 212-777-9515 or 800-222-0418.
www.wshotel.com.

Across Washington Square Park in Green-wich Village, this intimate 1902 property is introduced by the small lobby, with its hand-painted tile murals of wildflowers. Most rooms have been updated with a minimalist décor of mustard-colored walls and ebonized-wood night stands. **North Square ($$)** restaurant *(lower level)* is a secret neighborhood find.

Wolcott Hotel
$$ 169 rooms

4 W. 31st St. at Fifth Ave., Garment District. 212-268-2900. www.wolcott.com.

Just three blocks from the Empire State Building, this 1904 hotel offers elegance at a terrific price. Rooms are relatively large and well furnished, with air-conditioning, safes, WebTV, and Nintendo games. Free coffee and muffins are served every morning in the lobby, a soaring space with elaborately carved moldings and crystal chandeliers. Baggage lockers are available for early and late checkouts.

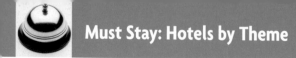

Another Way to Look at It: Hotels by Theme

Looking for a place that will welcome you and your two toddlers? How about one that will tolerate—nay, pamper—your darling chihuahua? In the previous pages we've organized the properties by price category; here we've arranged them by theme to help you find the perfect accommodations. All hotels listed below are in Manhattan.

Family Friendly
Excelsior Hotel (p 120)
Gershwin Hotel (p 122)
Hotel Belleclaire (p 122)
Hotel Chandler (p 120)
The Lucerne (p 121)
Ritz-Carlton NY, Central Park (p 116)

Hippest Decor
Hudson Hotel (p 121)
The Royalton (p 117)
Westin NY at Times Square (p 119)
W New York (p 119)

Hotels with History
Algonquin Hotel (p 117)
Hotel Belleclaire (p 122)
Hotel Chelsea (p 120)
Inn at Irving Place (p 116)
Waldorf-Astoria Hotel (p 117)

Hotels with Notable Bars
Algonquin Hotel (p 117)
Hudson Hotel (p 121)
The Mansfield (p 118)
The Royalton (p 117)
W New York (p 119)

Pets Welcome
Hotel 41 at Times Square (p 120)
Hotel 57 (p 118)
The Mansfield (p 118)
Ritz-Carlton NY, Central Park (p 116)
Westin New York (p 119)

Spa Experiences
Ritz-Carlton NY, Central Park (p 116)
Waldorf-Astoria Hotel (p 117)
Westin NY at Times Square (p 119)

Downtown
Best Western Seaport Inn (p 122)
Cosmopolitan Hotel (p 122)
Gershwin Hotel (p 122)
Hotel Chelsea (p 120)
Inn at Irving Place (p 116)
Larchmont Hotel (p 122)
Manhattan Seaport Suites Hotel (p 123)
Washington Square Hotel (p 123)

Midtown
Algonquin Hotel (p 117)
Avalon (p 119)
Hotel Chandler (p 120)
Hotel 57 (p 118)
Hotel 41 at Times Square (p 120)
Hotel Pennsylvania (p 120)
Hudson Hotel (p 121)
Iroquois Hotel (p 118)
The Mansfield (p 118)
Mayfair New York (p 123)
New York Palace (p 118)
Pickwick Arms (p 123)
Ritz-Carlton NY, Central Park (p 116)
The Royalton (p 117)
Waldorf-Astoria Hotel (p 117)
Westin NY at Times Square (p 119)
W New York (p 119)
Wolcott Hotel (p 123)

Uptown
Amsterdam Inn (p 121)
Bentley Hotel (p 119)
Excelsior Hotel (p 120)
Hotel Belleclaire (p 122)
The Lucerne (p 121)

The following abbreviations may appear in this Index: NHP National Historical Park; NHS National Historic Site; NM National Monument; NMem National Memorial; NP National Park; SHS State Historic Site; SP State Park.

Index

MANHATTAN SUBWAYS

WORLD TRADE CENTER	Terminal station for line designated
C E	End of line (normal service)
◆	End of line (part-time service)
	Transfer station
BROADWAY NASSAU ST	Station name
Chambers St	
A·1	Full-time service
C·5	Part-time service
	Train station
✈	AirTrain connection

0   1/2mi
0   1km